Aircraft in Warfare: The Dawn of the Fourth Arm

Frederick William Lanchester

BIBLIOLIFE

Copyright © BiblioLife, LLC

BiblioLife Reproduction Series: Our goal at BiblioLife is to help readers, educators and researchers by bringing back in print hard-to-find original publications at a reasonable price and, at the same time, preserve the legacy of literary history. The following book represents an authentic reproduction of the text as printed by the original publisher and may contain prior copyright references. While we have attempted to accurately maintain the integrity of the original work(s), from time to time there are problems with the original book scan that may result in minor errors in the reproduction, including imperfections such as missing and blurred pages, poor pictures, markings and other reproduction issues beyond our control. Because this work is culturally important, we have made it available as a part of our commitment to protecting, preserving and promoting the world's literature.

All of our books are in the "public domain" and some are derived from Open Source projects dedicated to digitizing historic literature. We believe that when we undertake the difficult task of re-creating them as attractive, readable and affordable books, we further the mutual goal of sharing these works with a larger audience. A portion of BiblioLife profits go back to Open Source projects in the form of a donation to the groups that do this important work around the world. If you would like to make a donation to these worthy Open Source projects, or would just like to get more information about these important initiatives, please visit www.bibliolife.com/opensource.

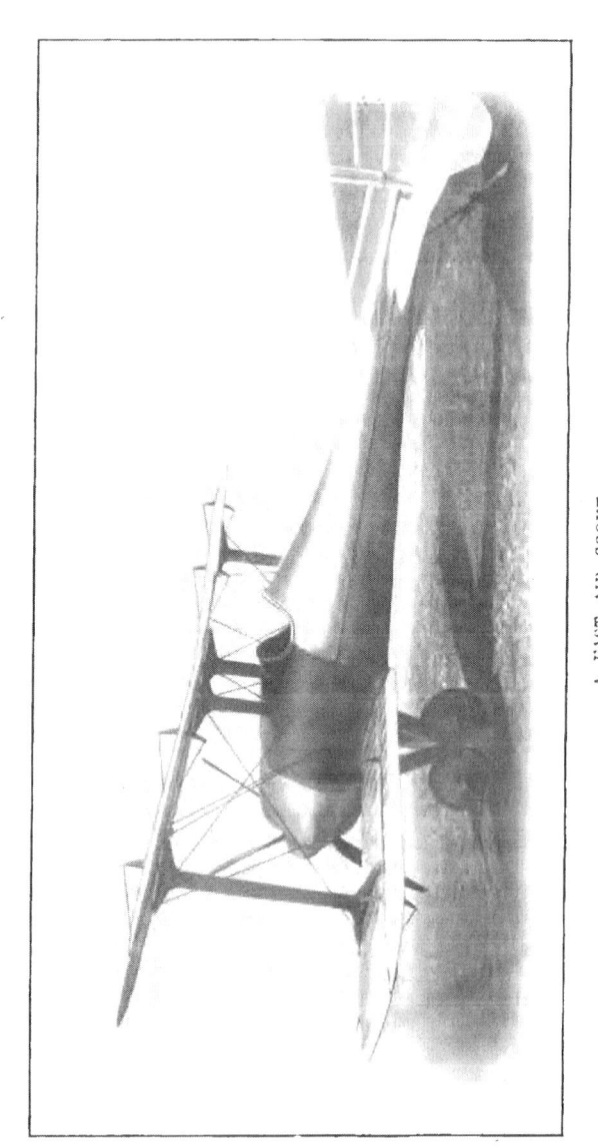

A FAST AIR SCOUT.
Compare Plate XIII.

AIRCRAFT
IN
WARFARE
THE DAWN OF THE FOURTH ARM

BY

F. W. LANCHESTER
M.INST.C E.   M.INST A.E.
MEMBER ADVISORY COMMITTEE FOR AERONAUTICS
AUTHOR OF "AERIAL FLIGHT" "AERODYNAMICS" "AERODONETICS"

WITH INTRODUCTORY PREFACE BY

AJ.-GEN. SIR DAVID HENDERSON, K
DIRECTOR GENERAL OF MILITARY AERONAUTICS

LONDON
CONSTABLE AND COMPANY LIMITED
ORANGE STREET LEICESTER SQUARE
1916

PREFACE.

The subject of "Aircraft in Warfare," with which Mr. Lanchester deals, is, and for some time will be, highly controversial. In each of its three aspects, the scientific, the military, and the material or manufacturing, it is still in the stage of experiment and speculation. The results obtained cannot always be made available for the information of the general public, and those which are available have usually been set forth in terms so technical, either in a scientific or a military sense, as to be somewhat difficult for the general reader to understand. Very little trustworthy information, therefore, has been disseminated, and the uninstructed public, hungry for information on a novel and alluring subject, of which the national importance is evident, has fallen an easy prey to the imposter. Any plausible rogue, gifted with sufficient assurance, and aided by a ready pen or supple tongue, has been able to pose as an "aeronautical expert," and to find some kind of following. To those who, as a matter of duty, or in search of information, have perused the aeronautical discussions carried on in the Press, or the reports of such discussions elsewhere, the very word "expert" calls up a strange procession of inventors, politicians, motor-trade touts, journalists, trick-fliers, novelists and financial agents, most of them, axe in hand, on the way to the national grindstone; a few, innocent, following on the same track, on a vague quest for supernatural powers of flight.

As a matter of fact, there are no experts in military aeronautics. There are experts in the various branches: in flying, in scientific research, in the design and construction of aeroplanes and engines, in military organisation and tactics. But, as yet, there is little opportunity for the expert in one branch to gain definite knowledge of the others, except by hard personal experience; in every direction there is progress, in every section of work opinion is fluid, and the views of the workers are not yet sufficiently crystallised to permit of definite instruction to others. Yet there are some students who, by reason of their receptive minds, and their wide and varied experience, have mastered so many of the fundamental problems that they are well qualified to review the general position, and to put forward a reasoned statement of their views. And of those so qualified, none has a wider view than Mr. Lanchester.

Of all the fields in which work for the advancement of military aeronautics has been undertaken, in this country, that of scientific research has, up to the present, produced the results that will probably be the most enduring. It is only by the solution of fundamental problems of science that improvement in the power of flight can be won. Solutions may be obtained, and some few have been, by chance, or by intuition; but to gain the full value of the result, it is necessary that the scientific solution should also be found, as a basis for further deductions. In this work of stating and solving the problems of aeronautics, Mr. Lanchester was one of the pioneers; he was bold enough to publish the result of his investigations at a time when flying had only just been proved possible; and he has reason now to be well satisfied with the quality of his early work. In this new book he has discussed matters of wide interest and, at the present moment, of vital importance, and has considered in many bearings the relations between aeronautic science and military art. In this effort many difficulties have had to be faced, not the least of which is the lack of definite knowledge of the methods which have been employed and of the results which have been achieved by aircraft in the present war. And, further, there has been the necessity of exercising extreme discretion in the use of information which is within his knowledge. In the first respect I have some advantage over Mr. Lanchester; in the second he, in writing the book, and I in introducing it, suffer under the same disability.

During the past three years Mr. Lanchester and I have had several tussles in private on the questions debated in this book. Each can put up a pretty good defence on his own ground. Mr. Lanchester is well protected by his profound knowledge of physical science and his practical acquaintance with several branches of engineering. I am strongly entrenched behind a barricade of military prejudice, with some dim recollections of early scientific training as reserves for counter-attack. In my incursions into Mr. Lanchester's territory, I have now and then received a buffet which has made me more wary. And occasionally, I think, Mr. Lanchester has found himself hung up in my wire entanglements. I should like nothing better than to fight out, in public and with due formality, these points—not a few—on which he and I disagree; but at the present moment this is impossible, nor is it advisable that I should do much towards indicating those on which we are in agreement.

There are two theories, however, evolved by Mr. Lanchester to which I may safely draw attention. The first he has called the *N-square* law, and it is, to my mind, a most valuable contribution to the art of war. It is the scientific statement of a truth which, although but dimly perceived, has been skilfully used by many great captains, both Naval and Military, but it is now for the first time stated in figures and logically proved. We can never be governed by the rules of exact science; there are too many conflicting factors, too many fortuitous circumstances; but there are certain rules, whether based on experience or calculation, which no commander may lightly transgress. Concentration of force is one of these rules, and a statement of the inevitable disadvantages of dispersion is valuable. The examples chosen from sea and land warfare illustrate the working of the law with admirable precision.

In the other case, Mr. Lanchester's calculations are less satisfactory. In considering the proportion of aircraft which is suitable for the requirements of an army in the field, the aircraft are compared with cavalry, and the aeroplane with a single trooper. This is no sound basis for calculation. To begin with, a single aeroplane absorbs, on the average, the services of some twelve officers and men, and its cost, which is not an immaterial factor, would provide more than a score of horses. But even the most accurate display of comparative figures will bring us no nearer to a correct result. The aeronautical arm is a new force in war, performing new functions, extending its activities every day and, at present, recognising but few limitations to its possible development. There is, as yet, no rule-of-thumb method of arriving at a definite and correct allotment of aircraft to an army of given strength. The only safe line on which to proceed is to consider, first, what are the services which the aircraft are to be required to perform? Second, how much of our available resources are we justified in devoting to these services? The answer to the first question shows a list which increases with each successive month of war. The mere propounding of the second will inevitably raise a controversy of which the only possible settlement will be a compromise. The final decision, however, ought to be based on relative value, not on relative numbers.

On the merits of these and other questions raised by Mr. Lanchester, the reader must be the judge. I hope that there may be many readers, and that they will give consideration to their judgments, for, whether they agree or not with the author, they will find here much that is worthy of study and reflection.

DAVID HENDERSON.

AUTHOR'S NOTE.

The Military and Naval importance of aeronautics, more especially of mechanical flight, has in the past been slow to receive adequate recognition. Even to-day, in spite of the awakening which has been brought about by the Great War, we are far from a full appreciation of the extent to which, as a nation, our destiny will be determined by aircraft and by military aeronautics.

The early pioneers of mechanical flight were but little concerned with the prospective future of flying; they were rightly occupied in overcoming the difficulties standing in the way of achievement. That ultimately a field of utility would present itself was generally accepted as an article of faith. Many suggestions both as to commercial and military usage were put forward, more frequently than not in ignorance of the limitations by which flight as a mode of locomotion is circumscribed: often claims were made of an altogether extravagant character. If it be true that in some directions, from the point of view of those early engaged in aeronautical development, the outlook has proved a disappointment, it is no less certain that military aeronautics has not only fulfilled, but already transcended, the most sanguine expectation.

Without going so far as to claim having predicted or foreseen in its entirety the many-sided utility of aircraft as it is to-day manifesting itself, the author can point to the fact that he has in the past taken every opportunity to insist on the importance of dynamic flight in its Military and Naval application. Thus, so long ago as 1897, in a patent specification* in which all the main features of the present day aeroplane were figured and discussed, the proposal is made for an air-borne torpedo, a device to which the first nine figures specifically relate.

Writing in 1907, in the preface to the first volume of his "Aerial Flight," the author expressed his view in a passage as follows :—

"The importance of this matter [provision for the scientific study of aerial flight] entitles it to rank almost as a National obligation; for the country in which facilities are given for the proper theoretical and experimental study of flight will inevitably find itself in the best position to take the lead in its application and practical development. That this must be considered a vital question from a National point of view is beyond dispute ; under the conditions of the near future the command of the air must become at least as essential to the safety of the Empire as will be our continued supremacy on the high seas."

And in 1909, the "Morning Post" (May 11th), reporting the 3rd Cantor Lecture delivered before the Royal Society of Arts, quotes the author as follows :—

" He considered that the immediate future of the flying machine was entirely confined to its military possibilities."

Again in the spring of 1914 (a few months prior to the outbreak of war) the author wrote :—†

" Without looking so far ahead as has been attempted in the preceding paragraph,‡ it cannot to-day be disputed

* No. 3608 of 1897.
† "James Forrest" Lecture. Proc. Inst. C. E., excviii., p. 251.
‡ The paragraph in question is that quoted incidentally on p. 158 of the present work.

AUTHOR'S NOTE. xiii.

that the immediate future of the flying-machine is guaranteed by its employment by the Army and Navy. It is already admitted by military and naval authorities that for the purpose of reconnaissance an aeronautical machine of some kind is imperative, and its more active employment as a gun-carrying or bomb- (or torpedo-) bearing machine will without question follow: its utility in this direction has already been experimentally demonstrated. In the author's opinion, there is scarcely an operation of importance hitherto entrusted to cavalry that could not be executed as well or better by a squad or fleet of aeronautical machines.* If this should prove true, the number of flying-machines eventually to be utilized by any of the great military Powers will be counted not by hundreds but by thousands, and possibly by tens of thousands, and the issue of any great battle will be definitely determined by the efficiency of the Aeronautical Forces."

In addition to the foregoing, the author gave especial prominence to military aeronautics, as presenting the most promising field of development, in his Presidential address† to the Institution of Automobile Engineers, in October, 1910.

The intention to write specifically on the subject of Aircraft in Warfare had been in the author's mind for some years, it was only after the outbreak of hostilities however that this intention came to be realised. The present work may be said to date from its contribution as a series of articles to "Engineering," covering a period from September to December, 1914. The text and order of the original articles have been preserved in the present volume, and thus the matter appears under the dates of its original publication. Revision

* Perhaps an overstatement of the case. Compare § 18.
† Proc. Inst. Automobile Engineers, Vol. V, p. 10.

xiv. AUTHOR'S NOTE.

has, in the main, been confined to ordinary legitimate corrections, the articles having been regarded and treated to all intents and purposes as a first proof. The last two chapters, however, include new matter; they are for this reason undated.

That it is at least desirable to give the dates of first publication is determined by the fact that the ever ready plagiarist commonly has one's writing over his own name almost before the ink of the original has had time to dry.* Beyond this the author has no wish to present as a *new edition*, matter which is more justly entitled to rank as a *reprint*; he has the satisfaction of knowing that articles in a technical journal, whatever its standing may be, can never appeal to so wide a circle as publication in book form.

* A coincidence such as the following scarcely requires comment.

From an article contributed by a certain writer to the "Westminster Gazette," February 25th, 1909 :—	From a paper read by the author December 8th, 1908, before the Aeronautical Society of Great Britain; as reported in "The Engineer," December 18th, 1908, and as subsequently published in the proceedings of the Society, January, 1909 :—
". . . that Lilienthal invented a gliding apparatus, which was improved in its structural features and in its method of control successively by Chanute and the Wright brothers, until the latter, by installing a comparatively light-weight motor and screw propeller, achieved, for the first time in history, a man-carrying machine propelled by its own motive power."	"The gliding machine originated by Lilienthal, was improved especially as to its structural features and its method of control, successively by Chanute and the Brothers Wright, until the latter, by the addition of a light-weight petrol motor, and screw propellers, achieved, for the first time in history, free flight in a man-bearing machine propelled by its own motive power."

Unfortunately, even though one may be morally certain as to the fact, it is not usually possible when broad opinions or the general results of an investigation are taken without acknowledgment, to "pillory" the offender, it is only when concerned with a quite trivial matter of words, as in the foregoing, that an accusation can be brought home. If such cases were clearly deliberate they would morally constitute a theft, since Editors commonly pay *according to the space filled*, but it is fair to assume that plagiarism of this kind is quite unconscious, what is read or heard one day, masquerades in the writer's mind as inspiration the next.

Occasionally one is fortunate, as the author when his theoretical method of treating the problem of the screw propeller was attributed to Drzewiecki in a report *in which the author's specially invented terminology was used throughout* Those who misappropriate another man's gold should take the ordinary precaution of throwing away the purse.

AUTHOR'S NOTE.

Looking back to the time at which the original articles were penned, it must be admitted that very great progress has been made, progress not only in the number and quality of the belligerent aeroplanes, but also more generally in the understanding of the potential capabilities of the Aeronautical Arm; the author finds, however, that his own ideas also have developed and expanded; the experience gained has, in a sense, cleared our vision, and enabled us to look still further into the future. Thus, in spite of the great advance, the pressing needs of the future seem in no wise diminished.

The author in conclusion desires to acknowledge his debt of gratitude to Maj.-Gen. Sir David Henderson, K.C.B., to whom the preface of the present volume is due. He counts himself singularly fortunate in having been accorded the support of so great an authority on Military Aeronautics, and feels confident that his gratitude will be shared by those into whose hands this book may fall.

Birmingham,
November, 1915.

CONTENTS.

CHAPTER I.
Aircraft as Constituting a New or Fourth " Arm."
Primary and Secondary Functions of the Aeronautical Arm.

CHAPTER II.
Aeroplane *versus* Airship or Dirigible—Speed Limitations.
Aeroplane and Dirigible in Armed Conflict.
Means of Attack and Defence.

CHAPTER III.
Strategic and Tactical Uses of the Aeronautical Arm.
The Strategic Scout and its Duties.
Directing Artillery Fire by Aircraft.
Aircraft as Vulnerable to Gun-fire.
Armour and Altitude as Means of Defence.

CHAPTER IV.
Low Altitude Flying.
The Aeroplane in a Combatant Capacity—Armour Plate.
The Machine Gun in the Service of the Aeronautical Arm.
The Fighting Type of Aeroplane and its Future.
As Affecting the Cavalry Arm.

CHAPTER V.
The Principle of Concentration.
The Value of Numerical Strength.
The *N-Square* Law.

CHAPTER VI.
The Principle of Concentration—*Continued.*
The *N-Square* Law in its Application.
Applications of the *N-Square* Law in Naval Warfare.
British Naval Tactics in 1805.
Nelson's Tactical Scheme—The *N-Square* Law at Trafalgar.

CHAPTER VII.

Attack by Aeroplane on Aeroplane.
The Fighting Machine as a Separate Type.
The Question of Armament—Treaty Restrictions.
Importance of Rapid Fire—Machine Guns Multiply Mounted.

CHAPTER VIII.

Rapidity of Fire and its Measure.
Armour in its Relation to Armament.
Importance of Upper " Gage "—Attack from Above
Armour and Shield Protection.

CHAPTER IX.

Gun-fire Ballistics—The Energy Account.
Expanding and Explosive Bullets.
Theory of the Expanding Bullet.
The Light-weight Shell.

CHAPTER X.

Miscellaneous Weapons and Means of Offence.
The Bomb and the Hand Grenade.
Bomb Dropping, Difficulties of Aiming.
Rockets, Air-borne Torpedoes, etc.
Supremacy of the Gun against Aircraft.

CHAPTER XI.

Aircraft in the Service of the Navy—Naval Reconnaissance.
Mother-ship or Floating Base.
Armament of the Naval Aeroplane—the Employment of Bombs.
Torpedo Attack by Air.
Aeroplane and Submarine—Attack by Bomb.

CHAPTER XII.

Aircraft in the Service of the Navy—*Continued*.
The Naval Air-scout.
The Flying-Boat Type—The Double Float Type.
The Ocean-going Floating Base or Pontoon-ship.

CHAPTER XIII.

The Command of the Air.
Air Power as Affecting Combined Tactics.
Defeat in the Air an Irreparable Disaster.
Employment of Aircraft in Large Bodies—Air Tactics.

CHAPTER XIV.

An Independent Combatant Air Fleet and its Duties.
Tactical Importance of Altitude.
Formation Flying—Airmanship and Signalling.
The " V " Formation and its Value.
Aircraft Bases at High Altitude.

CHAPTER XV.

The Command of the Air and its Limitations.
Belligerent Aircraft and the Rights and Obligations of Neutrals.
Other International Questions Relating to Aircraft.
Aircraft in Neutral Territory.

CHAPTER XVI.

Present Day Position—The Fourth Arm in Peace Time.
The Flight Ground Question—Depreciation and Obsolescence.
British Ascendancy in the Air.
Causes which have Contributed to British Ascendancy.
The Advisory Committee for Aeronautics.
The Royal Aircraft Factory.

CHAPTER XVII.

The Maintenance of British Supremacy.
Government *versus* Private Manufacture.
Continuity of Policy—A Scheme of Control.
A Board of Aeronautics Advocated.

CHAPTER XVIII.

Retrospect—The Scope and Limitations of the Work.
Supplementary Notes on the *N-Square* Law.
Air Raids and the Value of Numbers.
A Further Note on Aircraft and Submarine.
The Strategic Employment of Aircraft on a Large Scale.

CHAPTER XIX.

Air Raids—Some Questions of National Defence.
Power of Aggression as Affected by Radius of Action.
Air Raids as Affecting the Naval Outlook.
Aeronautical and Naval Defence Indissolubly Associated.
Future of Air Power : Essentially a National Question.
Categorical Statement of Recommendations for Future Policy.

LIST OF PLATES.

PLATE		PAGE
	Frontispiece.	
I.	R.A.F. Type B.E.2. As flown at the International Competition in August, 1912	4
II.	Field Tent for Aeroplane; Back View	12
III.	R.A.F. Type B.E.2c. Fitted with R.A.F. (British Built) Engine	20
IV.	Skeleton of Type B.E.2. Showing position of Tank, Seats, Engine, and Body structure	28
V.	Test of "Bullet-Proof" Steel Plate, 3 m.m. thick	36
VI.	R.A.F. Type F.E.2. Designed to carry gun weight 300 lbs.	68
VII.	R.A.F. Type R.E.5. An "R.E. Portable" Tent Pole used as Derrick for dismounting Engine	76
VIII.	"Flying Boat" Type. Built by Messrs. White and Thompson	108
IX.	Hydro-Aeroplane H.R.E.3. R.A.F. Design for the "Naval Wing" in 1912	108
X.	Floats 1912 Type, as fitted to H.R.E.3	116
XI.	R.A.F. Type R.E.1. (1912) Folded for Transport or Storage	124
XII.	An Example of Rough Usage. The Sopwith "Scout," a very fast single seater	158
XIII.	R.A.F. Type S.E.4. Single Seat Reconnaissance Machine	160
XIV.	Early (Experimental) Model of B.E.2c. Calculated and Demonstrated as inherently Stable by the late Mr. E. T. Busk	164

AIRCRAFT IN WARFARE
THE DAWN OF THE FOURTH ARM

CHAPTER I.

(*September 4th, 1914*)

AIRCRAFT AS CONSTITUTING A NEW OR FOURTH "ARM." THE PRIMARY AND THE SECONDARY FUNCTIONS OF THE AERONAUTICAL ARM.

§ 1 *Introductory.* All authorities may to-day be said to agree on the broad fact of the utility and importance of the flying-machine or aeroplane—or, more broadly, aircraft—in warfare; but at present the air service *as a fourth Arm* of the military organisation, either of this country or of any of the other great military Powers, can only be regarded as of a tentative and experimental character.

It is, unfortunately, not yet possible to draw conclusions of a lasting nature from the actual usage of aircraft in the present war, mainly for two reasons. Firstly, the machines at present available (with possibly a few exceptions) are entirely without armour or defence of any kind, and, dirigibles apart, are, generally speaking, without guns or other offensive armament of an effective character. Secondly, the machines are numerically so weak that, as an Arm of the Service, the aeronautical forces are a negligible factor. The question of sufficiency in numbers is evidently dependent upon the point of view

§ 1   AIRCRAFT IN WARFARE.

taken. On the one hand, if we regard the flying corps as merely the successor to the pre-existing balloon corps, the numbers, as they at present stand, may be regarded as sufficient; indeed, perhaps, even liberal. On the other hand, if we would recognise in the advent of the aeroplane the dawn of a fourth Arm (this being the point of view adopted by the author), the present strength, which in no case represents numerically one-twentieth part of 1 per cent. of the number of bayonets, is a truly negligible quantity. In order to get a fair perspective of the position, it is sufficient to institute a comparison with the cavalry, to which Arm, from its function, the aeronautical Arm is most closely akin; here the accepted numerical proportion in a modern army is about 6 per cent. Now there are many otherwise competent authorities who would deny to the aeroplane (or to aircraft generally) the potential importance which the author hopes satisfactorily to demonstrate is its due; let us put the matter to the test. We hear frequent reports of the work done by German aircraft, and particularly the effective tactical reconnaissance of the German aeroplanes, which appear to be continuously employed during the course of every engagement for locating our gun positions, directing gun-fire, following up bodies of troops in retreat, etc. We also hear reports of their wider field of operations, presumably reconnoitring the strategic distribution of the forces of the Allies at points remote from the enemy's lines. We may presume that the Belgian, French, and British aircraft are employed with equal success; but here, in the nature of things, the information which appears in our Press is meagre. As already pointed out, the total number of machines engaged is microscopic; the Germans are reputed to have possessed at the outbreak of hostilities some 500 machines in all. If the German cavalry had been limited to 500 mounted men, would it have proved of any real utility? Answer is unnecessary. It may be reasonably argued that the capital value of an aeroplane, with pilot and observer, being so much greater than that of a cavalryman, the above comparison is unfair; granting this objection, the position is not seriously altered, the equivalent force would be quite unperceived and be of no tangible service to the German army of to-day.

If, then, instead of the present moment being that of the introduction of the aeroplane (and dirigible), it had chanced to be the moment when mounted men were put on trial for the first time as a fighting force, and presuming the initial trial to have been made on a similarly modest scale, the mounted men would, relatively speaking, have proved a failure, and no one, not possessed of exceptional intuition or foresight, would have had the least conception of the possibilities of cavalry when numerically sufficient, boldly handled in masses and with appropriate supports.

The foregoing does not constitute a demonstration that the air service is in the future destined to become as important an auxiliary to an army in the field as the cavalry of to-day, although this is in effect the belief of the present author. Clearly, if we may judge from the scale of preparation which obtains, it is far from being the accepted view, in this country at least. The difficulty in connection with the present subject is that in order to get the future into true perspective, it is necessary to be able to look forward along two parallel lines of development—*i.e.*, to visualise the improvement of aircraft possible in the near future as a matter of engineering development, and simultaneously to form a live conception of what this improvement and evolution will open up in the potentialities of the machine as an instrument of war. The author does not wish it to be supposed that he is

§ 1   AIRCRAFT IN WARFARE.

endeavouring to lay down complete axioms as to the military future of aircraft of a positive character, or that he pretends to be in a position to formulate a cut-and-dried constructive programme; his intention is rather to give something in the nature of a lead in the direction in which it appears development may be logically anticipated.

§ 2. *The Primary and Secondary Functions of the Aeronautical Arm.* It is generally recognised that in its employment in connection with military operations a most valuable property of the flying-machine or aeroplane is its mobility; it is mobile to a degree which can scarcely have been dreamt of in the warfare of the past. When, therefore, we look for uses in co-operation with an army in the field in which the aeroplane may show to advantage, we naturally turn to examine the duties at present fulfilled by the cavalry, hitherto the Arm to be employed wherever mobility is of importance. Thus it is well recognised that one of the main duties for which the cavalry have hitherto been responsible—namely, reconnaissance—is a duty to which aircraft are pre-eminently suited. It is at the outset important to realise that cavalry, in face of the improvements in small arms and artillery,* with the advent of the armoured motor-car, and with the greater mobility of the main bodies of troops in modern warfare, have been finding the difficulties of effective reconnaissance continually on the increase. It is stated by one of the greatest authorities on the subject that of the reports sent in by cavalry patrols not more than 1 per cent. are of any use to the commanding officer, usually owing to events having anticipated the receipt of the information; in other words, the whole process of tactical recon-

* Not to mention entanglements of barbed wire.

4

PLATE 1.

R.A.F. TYPE B.E.2. As flown at the International Competition in August, 1912. The forerunner of the later B.E.2 Types. Speed: Max. 70 m/h.; not inherently stable.

naissance by cavalry has become far too slow to keep pace with the conditions of modern war.

So far as the author is aware, there has, up to the present, been no serious attempt to work out in complete detail the duties which can be undertaken by aircraft, or to define in specification form by any process of logic the types of machine which will be necessary at the outset to deal with the various duties so postulated. It is necessary to say *at the outset*, in view of the fact that if to-day we had a perfect organisation based on existing conditions, the first great Power to be similarly equipped would require to be answered in the form of a further equipment especially directed to his destruction, and so (as in the evolution of the Navy) we may in due time have aerial destroyers and "super" destroyers, and again still faster and more heavily-armed machines for the destruction of these.

The primary function of, and basic justification for, any Arm is the execution of its duties in relation to other than its own kind; thus, although it is admittedly one of the first and most important duties of cavalry to drive the enemy's cavalry out of the field, and establish ascendency, this is actually the secondary function of the cavalry Arm; its primary function is the observation and harrying of the other Arms of the Service. Again, the primary function of a fleet is neither to hold nor defeat a hostile fleet, although this, its secondary function, is universally admitted to be its first and most important objective. Ultimately, in every case, there must be some primary purpose which gives rise to the need for any kind of fighting machine, apart from its power of offence or defence against its own kind; it is this primary purpose that imparts the initial impulse and direction to its development.

It is proposed forthwith to define the primary

function of the aeronautical Arm as comprised by its duties and actions relating to the three pre-existing Arms of the Service—viz., the infantry, cavalry, and artillery.[*] Its secondary function is defined as comprised by its duties in the attack on and defence from its like Arm—*i.e.*, the destruction or countering of hostile aircraft.

It is necessary to be perfectly clear as to the above definitions. In considering, in the first instance, the comparative merits of the aeronautical and the older Arms of the Service for any particular duty, as it is needful to do in order to justify, or otherwise, any particular type or usage, it is futile to import into the initial discussion the action or possible counter-manœuvres of the enemy's aircraft; this latter may, or may not, eventually prove an important factor, but its influence, when taken into account, must be studied not only as touching the air service in contemplation, but also at the same time as affecting the other Arms of the Service (more particularly the cavalry) in its corresponding usage. In brief, as a matter of logic, in discussing the functions and duties of the aeronautical Arm, and the type-specifications of machines by which its objects are to be secured, the primary function alone has to be considered. Subsequently, when a provisional scheme and specifications have been formulated, it is time to take count of the secondary function, and to endeavour by careful prevision to forestall the enemy.

---

[*] Also the Navy and merchant marine where naval warfare is in question.

CHAPTER II.
(September 4th, 1914).

AEROPLANE *versus* AIRSHIP OR DIRIGIBLE.

§ 3. *Aeroplane and Dirigible: Speed Limitations.* Two questions are involved in the consideration of the relative merits of the aeroplane and dirigible. We are firstly concerned with their respective advantages and disadvantages in relation to their primary function—namely, as instruments of reconnaissance, attack, and defence; secondly, we have to take into account their secondary function—*i.e.*, their relative power of mutual destruction; the question whether, for example, either can drive the other from the field, or whether each may have its own *rôle* to play in securing and holding the command of the air.

Before going into either of these questions in detail it is convenient to review a few of the facts by which limitations are imposed on the ultimate performance of either type of aircraft. We must avoid falling into error by judging each too closely by its performance of to-day.

The all-important question of *speed* is a matter depending primarily on the lightness (*i.e.*, horse-power per given weight) of the prime mover, and the law of resistance. The horse-power per unit weight of motor is roughly the same whichever type of aircraft is in question, and any future advance in the art of motor construction tending to diminish weight will, we may presume, be equally available for either type. The laws of resistance of the aeroplane and dirigible are

§ 3   AIRCRAFT IN WARFARE.

well understood; in the case of the former the resistance is approximated by a curve $a\ a$, Fig. 1, representing the sum of a resistance following the V-*square* law and a constant; the latter (the dirigible) may be taken as following the V-*square* law implicitly, Fig. 1, $b\ b$.

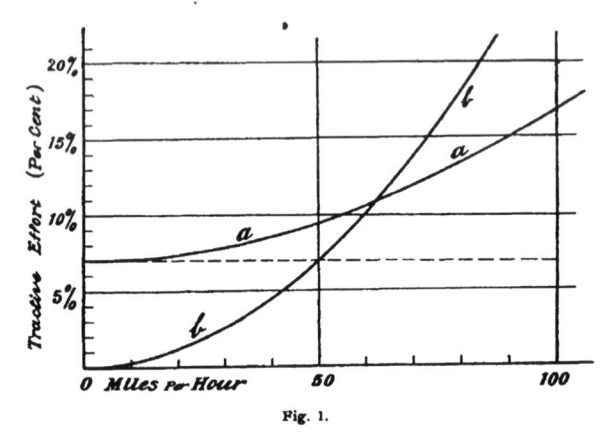

Fig. 1.

Fig. 1 represents approximately actual values of the resistance coefficients, in tractive effort per cent., in machines of average size as they exist to day, for the speeds given in miles per hour.*

One salient fact is at once evident; the greater the horse-power available for a given engine weight the greater the advantage in the matter of speed in favour of the aeroplane; the highest speed of flight of an aeroplane attained to-day (through, *i.e.*, relatively to, the air) is already more than twice that of which

* The maximum speed attained by an airship is approximately 50 miles per hour; the maximum in the case of an aeroplane is considerably over 100 miles per hour; thus (Fig. 1) the tractive coefficient in the case of the aeroplane is actually greater than in the case of the airship. The reason for this is that the dead-load in the airship—represented by the envelope and its appurtenances—is disproportionately great, and the proportion of the weight that can be devoted to the motive-power installation is relatively smaller than in the aeroplane. Were it not for this fact the airship would have held the advantage until speeds about 60 miles per hour had been reached and the aeroplane after.

the fastest dirigible is capable. There is every prospect that its advantage in this respect will increase rather than diminish with the march of progress.

Beyond the above, it is well understood that an increase in size is conducive to a reduction in the resistance coefficient; this applies, to both aeroplane and dirigible. This fact has been one of the controlling considerations in dirigible design; no dirigible, other than of comparatively large size, has been found to be of real service. It is, moreover, evident that, in the case of some of the large Zeppelins, it will not be found practicable to go very much further in the direction of increase. Here again the aeroplane is at an advantage ; we can in nowise regard the aeroplane of to-day as defining the limit.

It is abundantly manifest therefore that the dirigible is at a permanent disadvantage of not less than two to one in the matter of speed.

§ 4. *Aeroplane and Dirigible: other points of comparison.* The question of *range* and *duration* of flight is largely determined by petrol-carrying capacity. In the aeroplane both range and duration depend definitely upon the petrol supply holding out; in the case of the dirgible the same applies to a limited extent ; but here the duration and, to a less extent, the distance can be greatly prolonged by reducing the speed to the minimum possible without jeopardising the control. In the dirigible the gradual loss of buoyancy, due to the leakage and escape of hydrogen, is an independent determining factor.; Taking everything into account there is not much to choose between the two types of aircraft in the matter of range or radius of action ; on the other hand, under favourable conditions, the dirigible has undoubtedly the advantage on the score of duration of flight. The maximum is about 24 hours in

§ 4 AIRCRAFT IN WARFARE.

the case of the aeroplane, against 48 hours in the case of the dirigible. This may be taken as a fair indication of their relative capacity, though of no quantitative value as a guide to what is to be expected under service conditions. The possibilities of the future are here rather in favour of the airship; there is an absolute limit both of range and duration where the aeroplane is concerned.

On the question of *storage* or *housing* the advantage of the aeroplane is overwhelming; the aeroplane, especially if furnished with folding wings, can be stowed away in any ordinary shed or barn, or may be anchored in the open without serious risk, whereas the "balloon hall" necessary for the safety of an airship is not only costly, but is an unmistakable landmark for hostile aircraft at 20 miles distance. Again, bad weather affects the storage of an aeroplane but little, whereas the housing or getting out of an airship in a strong wind is a difficult and risky business, even under the best of conditions. A large Zeppelin may sometimes call for the services of 300 men.

The foregoing by no means exhausts the grounds of comparison, but is sufficient for the present purpose. It is scarcely necessary to point out the very great disparity of weight, and, incidental thereto, carrying capacity, between the two classes of machine; the large German Zeppelins have a gross weight, taken from their displacement, of 22 tons (military) up to 35 tons (naval); of the aeroplanes in service, practically all the military machines are less than 1 ton "tare," and most types do not exceed 1 ton gross—*i.e.*, with full complement, petrol, oil, etc.

If we were concerned with the primary function of the aeronautical arm alone, there appears to be no reason to doubt that both kinds of aircraft would have their place; the large air-ship has unquestionable

AEROPLANE AND DIRIGIBLE. § 4

advantages under suitable conditions: cruising at high altitudes over the battlefield, or over or in the rear of the enemy's lines, and reporting to headquarters by wireless every movement of strategic or tactical importance, it might render the most vital service. It is able to carry a complement of officers trained to observation, capable of giving an accurate interpretation of what they observe, and acting under most favourable conditions, such as are not possible in any existing aeroplane; it can move at some fifty miles per hour, if required, or remain to all intents and purposes stationary; it can follow continuously the course of events from sunrise to sunset, and remain the whole time in touch with headquarters, either for sending or receiving. On the other hand, for bearing despatches, for flying at low altitude within range of shot and shell, as may be necessary for detail reconnaissance or in cloudy or misty weather, for bringing machine-gun fire to bear at some important point or at a critical moment, etc., all these are duties for which the aeroplane is pre-eminently suited, as also for rapidly locating and signalling gun positions, directing fire, and duties of such-like character.

It is more than questionable whether actual fighting is any part of the primary function of a dirigible at all; it is at least becoming apparent that bomb-dropping is an entire misuse of the large airship; the results are incomparably small in view of the means employed, and can never affect decisively the course of any battle or campaign.

It is important to note that though it is possible effectively to armour an aeroplane, at least to be proof against small-arms fire, and that in any case the vulnerable target is small, the dirigible, presenting a mark larger than the proverbial haystack, cannot be effectively

§ 4   AIRCRAFT IN WARFARE.

protected. In spite of the fact that injury to the envelope is not necessarily dangerous, it has been reported that such injury has already necessitated a hurried descent into a hostile country, with the effective loss of both vessel and crew. These are the considerations which place the dirigible at a formidable disadvantage when within reach of the enemy's guns.

§ 5. *Aeroplane and Dirigible, analogy between Air and Naval Forces not tenable.* We may now pass to the discussion of the secondary function of the aeronautical Arm in its present relation—that is to say, we shall consider the question of aeroplane *versus* dirigible in armed conflict.

At the outset it is desirable to dispose of the much-worried analogy that crops up again and again when the present subject is discussed. Some of the most strenuous supporters of the airship as an auxiliary to the aeronautical service are fond of drawing a parallel between the air service and the Navy, the airship being put forward as analogous or comparable to the battleship or battle-cruiser, and the aeroplane to the torpedo boat or destroyer. In the author's opinion any such analogy is totally fallacious. The effective area of the target presented by an aeroplane is but a few square feet. The effective target area of a torpedo boat or destroyer is more than one hundred times as great. The time during which an aeroplane is visible and under fire, owing to its small size and high speed, is short compared to that of torpedo craft at sea.* The armament which a Zeppelin can bring to bear on an attacking aeroplane is confined to that which she can carry on a platform arranged on top of the structure, since the hostile aeroplane making its attack from above

* Added to this, in order to detect the approach of a hostile aeroplane, the sky has to be scanned in the three dimensions of space.

PLATE II.

FIELD TENT FOR AEROPLANE: BACK VIEW. Supported by two poles only; Roof ridge formed by stretched wire rope. *Designed R.A.F. 1913.*

AEROPLANE *VERSUS* DIRIGIBLE.   § 5

can manœuvre to remain in billiard phraseology, "snookered" so far as the gondolas and their armament are concerned. Beyond the above, the speed of the aeroplane is approximately double that of the airship, whereas the speed of a fast destroyer is not more than 25 or 30 per cent. superior to that of a fast and heavily-armoured cruiser or battleship of modern type, and even this advantage is lost in heavy weather.

It will be realised in considering the above facts that the whole analogy breaks down—the continued existence of the battleship or cruiser in the face of torpedo-craft does not in the least degree imply or involve the continuance of the airship as a logical probability.

September 11th, 1914.

§ 6. *Aeroplane and Dirigible in Armed Conflict.* Having in the preceding sections devoted some attention to contrasting the respective merits and limitations of the aeroplane and airship or dirigible, and to disposing of the false analogy so frequently drawn between the air forces and the Fleet, we pass to the consideration in greater detail of their mutual relationship in matters of attack and defence. Firstly, it is evident that the attack will essentially be on the side of the aeroplane; the dirigible can do no more than act on the defensive. The great disparity of speed alone, whatever armament the airship may carry, settles this definitely; it is within the power of the aeroplane to choose precisely when, how, and where it will engage in conflict. The dirigible, like the submarine, is too slow to run the enemy to earth or to bring him to bay, and, to its disadvantage, cannot, like the submarine, make itself invisible and attack by stealth. Beyond this, its quarry (the aeroplane) is of small size, often scarcely visible at a mile or two distance, and when not actually in the air can be either concealed

§ 6   AIRCRAFT IN WARFARE.

or efficiently protected. Any attempt at aggressive action on the part of the dirigible is totally and completely out of the question; it is, in fact, beyond the conceivable range of possibility.

On the other hand, if the airship is to continue as a factor in warfare at all, it must be able to defend itself against hostile aircraft, and in particular be capable of repelling the attack of the enemy's aeroplanes. Now the only power of defence possessed by a dirigible when attacked by an aeroplane is counter-attack by gun-fire; hence the extent, character, and distribution of its gun armament is one of the most important factors in its design.

In the earlier days of the development of the aeroplane when its horse-power was but little in excess of the minimum required for the bare necessities of flight, its rate of ascent was so extremely slow (if it could be said to have any real rate of ascent at all) that it was commonly assumed that a dirigible, or airship, could seek safety in altitude. To-day, however, many aeroplanes will make altitude at a speed of 700 ft. or 800 ft. per minute, thus being more than able to hold their own with the lighter-than-air machine, and can ascend to over 10,000 ft. altitude (even twice this height has been reached); again having the dirigible at a disadvantage.

§ 7. *Aeroplane* versus *Dirigible, means of Attack and Defence.* The method by which an aeroplane may most effectively attack a dirigible is a matter that remains for future experience to settle. If the aeroplane pilot is prepared to sacrifice himself, and has at his disposal a powerful machine of modern design, no dirigible can stand against him. Thus, if, as a matter of experience in actual service, men are found of sufficient grit and grim determination to adopt ramming tactics, and to hurl themselves and their craft bodily at the

AEROPLANE *VERSUS* DIRIGIBLE. § 7

gas-bag of the dirigible, its destruction is immediate and complete. There is no defence possible against this mode of attack. The crew of the dirigible may not have even the most slender chance of stopping the aeroplane by machine-gun fire; 'the attack can be made from above by a steep *vol plané* or a vertical dive. In the case of a large airship of the Zeppelin type, even with machine guns mounted "on the roof," the chances of defeating such an attack are remote; the speed of a machine descending vertically, or steeply, is approximately that of its limiting velocity—commonly about 150 miles per hour—leaving a very brief period in which to score a hit. Beyond this, no ordinarily fatal hit is effective under the conditions in question; no injury to the motive-power installation is of the least effect as a stopper, and the pilot is in almost perfect security in his position behind the engine. If by an exceptional chance he should be wounded, he is still able to effect his purpose, unless totally disabled.

The steep or vertical descent is admittedly a dangerous feat of airmanship, but it is not intrinsically dangerous; the risk involved is due to the structural stresses to which the machine is subjected when "flattening out." These, it is well known, may become excessive; any objection on the score of danger has obviously no weight whatever under the conditions contemplated.

It is an open question whether airmen will be found ready to step forward at the critical moment to go to certain death, and so the general feasibility of ramming tactics must for the time being remain in doubt. However, there are many other modes of attack open to the aeroplane pilot, all more or less untried at present; unquestionably also there are still other methods that will in due course be devised. In the case of the non-rigid dirigible, as in the ordinary spherical balloon, it is almost

§ 7 AIRCRAFT IN WARFARE.

certain that a hundred or so yards of barbed wire trailed beneath an aeroplane would be a quite sufficient weapon; equally effective would be an incendiary shell, or a rocket, presuming any part of the envelope to be hit. Ordinary small-arm or machine-gun fire is comparatively ineffective, since the bullet holes are, in any case, small, and in some of the modern machines repairs can be effected without coming to earth. However, even rifle fire has proved sufficient to bring a balloon down. It is evident that the weak point of any dirigible or airship is its liability to attack from above; in the non-rigid type, without going to the length of any elaborate apparatus, and without endangering the attacking aeroplane, almost *any* angular and weighty object dropped from a height cannot fail to be of conclusive effect if it fairly hits the envelope, and likewise in the case of the rigid type—such as the Zeppelin—the structure would not stand up under a blow from, say, a steel bar of any ordinary stock section of 70 lb. or 80 lb. weight dropped from a height of 200 ft. or 300 ft. Without saying that the above are suitable methods of attack, it may be claimed that they fairly indicate the inherent weakness of the dirigible in face of attack by an aeroplane of sufficient power to master it in the matter of altitude. There are methods not mentioned here which are actually in use or in contemplation, but which, for obvious reasons, require to be treated as confidential. It is, however, in the author's opinion, quite unnecessary to carry the matter further; the weaknesses of the dirigible on the defensive are so great and of such a character as to render it quite unfit to remain an active participant in aerial warfare. It may escape for a time, and may render a certain amount of useful service, but only thanks to the circumstance the number of high-powered, fast-climbing aeroplanes is comparatively limited, and to the fact that scientific methods of attack have not

AEROPLANE *VERSUS* DIRIGIBLE. § 7

yet been fully worked out or put into practice. However, even to-day, the finest of Germany's fleet of Zeppelins would be absolutely at the mercy of a modern aeroplane in the hands of a man prepared to make his one and last sacrifice. So fragile and combustible a contrivance as a dirigible, whether rigid, or non-rigid, can never, in the author's opinion, survive in the face of the rapid development of the aeroplane and the engines of offence with which before long it will be furnished.

Before proceeding to the broader considerations, it has been thought desirable to dispose of the airship as a factor in the aeronautical service—its dismissal being an initial simplification. It is not altogether important whether or not this conclusion turns out to be literally true. It may be that, in spite of all that has been put forward, the large airship may retain some degree of utility; even if this be so, the main conclusions will be unaffected. It is the aeroplane, and the aeroplane only, either as a reconnaissance or a fighting machine, acting independently or in flights or squadrons, which will in effect constitute the aeronautical Arm; and whether the considerations we discuss are strategic or tactical, it is the potential capabilities and limitations of the aeroplane that we require to keep constantly in mind.

CHAPTER III.
(September 11th, 1914).

STRATEGIC AND TACTICAL USES OF THE AERO-
NAUTICAL ARM. AIRCAFT AS VULNERABLE TO
GUN-FIRE. ARMOUR AND ALTITUDE AS MEANS
OF DEFENCE.

§ 8. *Strategic and Tactical Uses of the Aeronautical Arm.* In the present distribution of the cavalry Arm, the distinction between the strategic and tactical uses of cavalry is clearly recognised. For purely tactical purposes it is customary to attach one or more squadrons, usually a regiment of cavalry, to each infantry division. The main cavalry force on the other hand,—known as the independent cavalry,—constitutes a separate command, taking general instructions from the headquarters staff. The independent cavalry may be engaged in operations of strategic import, as in the conduct of a reconnaissance in force, or in the execution of a wide turning or out-flanking movement, or in the countering of such a movement on the part of the enemy. Alternatively it may be employed in its tactical capacity, its full weight being thrown at some critical moment into the fighting line, it may be to attack and destroy the cavalry of the enemy, to raid and capture or put out of action his artillery, to harass him in retreat, or to convert a retreat into a rout. The *divisional* cavalry are, generally speaking, employed for the latter—tactical—duties only.

In a similar manner aircraft are capable of employment in duties of both strategic and tactical import, and

STRATEGIC AND TACTICAL USES.　　§ 8

accordingly will probably need to be divided into divisional and independent commands. Thus there is the machinery of strategic reconnaissance, whose function it is to inform the headquarters staff of the main disposition and movements of the enemy's forces, positions of his depôts, magazines, etc., points of concentration and strength of his reserves, and last, but not least, his main and perhaps auxiliary lines of communication. On the tactical side there are similarly many duties to be carried out, analogous to those at present performed by cavalry; there are also duties which must be regarded as new, brought into being by the peculiar power and capacity of the aeronautical Arm; these are, in the main, such as would indicate control by the divisional command.

§ 9. *The Strategic Scout and its Duties.* The strategic value of the aeroplane depends mainly upon its utility for the purpose of reconnaissance; briefly it is its value as an informer, rather than as a fighter, that is of service to the headquarters staff. The duties of a machine thus acting are necessarily of an entirely different character from those of a machine employed in the minor operations of the field, whether for tactical scouting, direction of gun-fire, or otherwise. Firstly, the flight range or radius, as determined by petrol capacity, is a far more important factor in its design, since it will require to operate over a large area, and to cover long distances over the enemy's territory, where any renewal of fuel supply is impossible; secondly, its flight speed must be such as to render it reasonably secure against pursuit. Anything serious in the direction of armour or armament will be entirely out of place, since under no circumstances will such a machine be required to act in a combative capacity; its defence lies in its speed. It appears from all reports that the duties in question are such as to require an observer (probably a staff officer)

§ 9 AIRCRAFT IN WARFARE.

of mature knowledge from a military standpoint, with considerable flying experience, possessing something of an intuition for reading the meaning of the incomplete and fragmentary indications which are obtainable from high altitude observation. It is evidently not impossible for a strategic scout (as we may term the machine under discussion) to descend to low altitude in pursuit of more accurate and precise information; but it is always to be remembered that any such manœuvre is dangerous to an unarmoured machine; it may be too easily shot down or destroyed by shrapnel. In this latter event it must be regarded as having failed in its purpose. The possession of a wireless installation may be assumed, but, in the event of the machine being lost, the fact that reports had already been transmitted to headquarters would in no way mean that the machine had completely fulfilled its mission.

The work done by the strategic scout thus comprises the gleaning of information hitherto only to be obtained by espionage or by a reconnaissance in force—that is to say, by a large force of cavalry with supports of horse artillery and infantry, often involving considerable fighting and loss. It is quite improbable that aeroplane scouting will prove an entire substitute for such reconnaissance; in may be said that cavalry can *feel* and *act* where the air-scout can only *see* and *report*, but, as a prelude to cavalry reconnaissance, and as an auxiliary thereto, the services of the strategic scout should prove of the utmost utility. It will, at least, enable the cavalry force acting at a distance from its base, frequently in the rear of the enemy, to keep in constant touch with headquarters, and thus relieve the despatch rider of one of his most difficult and dangerous tasks. In service of this character it would seem probable that a *flight* or *squadron* of aeroplanes would be temporarily or per-

PLATE III.

R.A.F. TYPE B.E.2c. Fitted with R.A.F. (British Built) Engine.
Compare Plate XIV.

AUXILIARY TO TACTICAL OPERATIONS. § 9

manently attached to the independent cavalry, as in the case of the supports representing the other two Arms of the Service. Under these circumstances the command of the combined force would remain, as at present, with the cavalry leader.

(September 18th, 1914).

§ 10. *The Aeroplane as an Auxiliary to Tactical Operations.* The aeroplane in its employment in connection with tactical operations finds itself under conditions entirely different from those discussed in the preceding section; its duties are of a more varied character, and involve flying at lower altitudes than are compatible with security. It is likely to be almost continuously under fire, and, according to some of the experiences of the present war, it has almost as much to fear in this respect from its friends as its foes. Whereas the strategic reconnaissance machine is able to perform all its most useful work at high altitude, and avoid as far as possible the attention of, or actual contact with, the enemy, and evade pursuit by flight; the tactical machine (acting under the divisional command), whether engaged in local reconnaissance or in locating or directing gun-fire, or in other duties, must be prepared at once to tackle the enemy, and, in brief, to interfere as much as possible with the hostile aeroplane service. Under certain circumstances the instructions will undoubtedly be to make the aircraft of the enemy the first objective.

It is more than probable that it is in connection with the varied duties which in the future must fall to the Fourth Arm in its tactical usage, that differentiation of type and specialisation will eventually become the most marked. At present practically no attempt in the direction of specialisation has taken place. It is true the different machines in service vary considerably, and those responsible for the construction and specification of

§ 10   AIRCRAFT IN WARFARE.

Service aeroplanes have already begun to talk of "reconnaissance machines" and "fighting machines;" but the distinction is one that has scarcely yet penetrated to the field of operations. When all has been said, differentiation of type must, from the Service standpoint, be looked upon as an evil, only to be justified when, and to the extent that, service conditions prove it to be necessary. So far even the broad distinction between machines for strategic reconnaissance and for tactical operations has scarcely been drawn or received recognition. The military aeroplane of to-day is something like the frontiersman's knife—made for nothing in particular, used for everything in general.

For the purpose of directing artillery fire the experience of the present war has shown the aeroplane to be effective almost beyond the most sanguine expectation. For this purpose it appears to have established its utility beyond question. Its duties in this respect may be regarded as a special branch of local reconnaissance, its function being to locate the objective and signal its whereabouts to the gun batteries to which it is attached; further to report and correct inaccuracies of fire. The exact mode or modes of signalling adopted do not so far appear to have been definitely disclosed. Some reports give the aeroplane as turning sharply when over the enemy's position; according to other accounts a smoke bomb of some kind is let fall to indicate the position to be attacked; other reports, again, mention lights as being used. It appears that lamps of sufficient power to be visible in daylight are actually being employed by the German aircraft. Possibly all these methods are in use experimentally, or different kinds of signals may be used for different purposes, to indicate initially the position, and subsequently to give corrections, either as to direction or range. Whatever the methods

TACTICAL VALUE OF AIRCRAFT.   § 10

employed may be (and the details do not much concern us at the moment), they seem to be quite effective, and, it may be presumed, very considerably increase the fighting value of the guns. More than this, the value of aeroplane work will be relatively greater the longer the range; in fact, it may in future be found possible to employ heavy artillery of long range under conditions where, without the help of the aeroplane, it would be comparatively useless. As an illustration, there is nothing to-day to prevent a long-range battery, well served by its aeroplanes, from effectively shelling an enemy without knowing in the least the character of its objective—*i.e.*, whether an infantry force or position, a body of cavalry, or the enemy's guns. In the present war the aeroplane appears to have been utilised by the German army, as a matter of regular routine, as an auxiliary to the artillery in the manner indicated. It has been reported again and again that the appearance of an aeroplane overhead has been the immediate prelude to the bursting of shrapnel, frequently the very first shell being so accurately placed as to indicate that the method of signalling, and, in fact, the whole performance, must have been well thought out and equally well rehearsed.

It is well understood that the determination of the distance of an aeroplane of *known size* with approximate accuracy is a matter of perfect simplicity. Thus, if the aeroplane be flying fairly overhead, or directly towards or away from the observer, and the span be a known dimension, then by measuring the optical angle presented by the span, the distance or range is given by simple proportion. For example, holding a foot-rule square in front of one at arm's length—approximately 20 in. from the eye—the span, known to be, say, 36 ft., subtends an angle represented by, say, $\frac{1}{2}$ in. on the scale;

§ 10   AIRCRAFT IN WARFARE.

the distance is $\dfrac{20 \times 36}{0.5}$ = 1440 ft. Using such rough-and-ready "apparatus," the degree of accuracy to be expected is not great; however, the author has found it quite sufficient to determine the altitude of a machine to within 5 or 6 per cent. of the truth. If for the observer's arm and foot-rule we substitute a low-powered telescope or binocular of, say, 2 or 3 diameters magnification, with micrometer cross-wires, with which to follow up the apparent reduction in span of a receding aeroplane, until some prearranged signal is given, the range could undoubtedly be determined easily within 2 or 3 per cent. At 1 mile distance this means a degree of accuracy represented by a maximum error of about 40 yards, or sufficient to enable shrapnel to be dropped right on the mark. Parenthetically, it may be pointed out that the same method will enable the range of a hostile aeroplane to be determined, provided the type be identified, and its leading dimensions are known; it also suggests the importance of not flying exactly towards or away from, or exactly broadside to, any position of the enemy guarded by counter-aircraft artillery; flying end on to the enemy is also to be deprecated on the ground of fixity of direction.

§ 11. *Attack by Gun-Fire.* An aeroplane operating in a hostile country is liable to attack by rifle and machine-gun fire, also by shell-fire from special anti-aeroplane artillery. It has comparatively little to fear from field artillery owing to the want of handiness of the ordinary field-gun. The "laying" of a field-piece is far too clumsy a business to permit of its effective use on so small and rapidly moving a target as presented by an aeroplane in flight, though it may be effective when used against a dirigible. With regard to rifle or machine-gun (small bore) fire, calculation shows that aircraft is abso-

ATTACK BY GUN-FIRE. § 11

lutely safe at an altitude of somewhat over 7000 ft.; it is in that region that the top of the trajectory lies for vertical shooting.

The duties of a strategic scout on long-distance work would, without doubt, permit of flying at such a high altitude, and it may be added that, although absolute immunity is not reached at less than about 7000 ft., a solitary aeroplane can only present a very unprofitable target at far lower altitudes. In fact, it may be taken that at, say, 5000 ft. or 6000 ft., the amount of small-arm ammunition required to bring down an aeroplane would be enormous. Not only has the velocity become so reduced as to render a "hit" capable of but little mischief, but the time of flight of the bullet, rising vertically to this altitude, would be about 8 or 9 seconds and the distance moved by the aeroplane 1000 ft., more or less. Therefore it would be necessary to fire into quite a different part of the heavens from that in which the aeroplane is seen, something akin to sighting into the Great Bear to hit the Pole Star. Beyond this the gyroscopic drift of a bullet fired vertically is nil, against some 30 ft. or 40 ft. under normal conditions;* also the error due to the earth's rotation is a matter of about 30 ft. westward, and cannot be allowed for without taking reference to the compass bearing. Taking all these things into account, it is evident that for the infantryman or gunner not specially trained, the task of bringing down an aeroplane flying at high altitude is no light one, especially when we recall the fact that for every inclination and bearing of the line of sight, the conditions differ. In designing the mounting of aeroplane-stopping artillery or machine-guns, it would be possible to render the sighting corrections for such items as gyroscopic

---

*The normal sighting of a match rifle is arranged partially to correct for the gyroscopic drift.

§ 11   AIRCRAFT IN WARFARE.

drift and earth's rotation automatic; this could be done without difficulty, and would mean the elimination of errors whose combined value may amount to something like 60 ft. at 6000 ft. altitude—*i.e.*, an angular magnitude represented roughly by the apparent diameter of the sun or moon.

The height to which aircraft artillery will carry is by no means subject to the same limitation as that of the small-bore machine-gun or rifle, the resistance of the air being many times greater than that due to gravity. Thus the ordinary rifle bullet, at 2,000 foot-seconds muzzle velocity, would carry to a height of over 60,000 ft. *in vacuo*, instead of approximately 7,000 ft. actual. If we take the case of a 1-pounder having the same velocity, its effective vertical range is well over 12,000 ft., and from that calibre upwards the range will, in practice, be more a question of the shell being properly directed than whether it will attain the height. At the best, firing from the ground at an aeroplane at high altitude, will require skilful gunnery, and when near the limit of the trajectory nothing but sheer good luck will render a hit effective. The angle of "lead" it is necessary to give to allow for the velocity of flight, as already stated, is one of the difficulties of high-altitude shooting. This angle is only constant so long as the velocity of the projectile is constant, assuming (as fairly represents the conditions) the flight speed not to vary; at extreme heights the velocity of the projectile has fallen so low that a very slight error in range-finding will be fatal to accuracy. The solution of this difficulty may be found in the employment of guns of about 3-in. bore—*i.e.*, a 12-pounder or 15-pounder, with the concurrent advantage of a full shrapnel charge, and, in shot-gun terminology, a larger killing circle. The obvious disadvantages, however, of artillery, in place of a light automatic or

DEFENCE FROM GUN-FIRE. § 11

machine gun, lie in its want of portability and its unhandiness, difficulties which may, in course of time, be overcome.

All things considered, it would appear probable that attack on aeroplanes at high altitude from the ground will be found impracticable, or at least uncommercial. Not only have we to reckon with the various considerations above discussed, but also with the fact that, in our climate at least, not more than one day in four is sufficiently clear to render high-altitude shooting possible, and though it is true that an aeroplane, to make observation, cannot remain above or in the clouds, it presents but a poor mark under bad weather conditions.

An aeroplane operating at high altitude will probably need to be hunted and driven off or destroyed by armed machines of its own kind.

§ 12. *Defence from Gun-Fire.* It is manifestly not possible for an aeroplane to perform all the duties required of it, in connection with tactical operations at high altitude,* and whenever it descends below 5,000 ft., or thereabouts, it is liable to attack from beneath; in fact, at such moderate altitudes it must be considered as being under fire—mainly from machine-gun and rifle—the whole time it is over or within range of the enemy's lines. Protection from the rifle bullet may be obtained in either of two ways; the most vital portions of the machine, including the motor, the pilot, and gunner, can only be effectively protected by armour-plate; the remainder of the machine, including the wing members, the tail members, and portions of the fusilage not protected by armour, also the controls, struts, and the propellor, can be so constructed as to be *transparent* to rifle fire—that is to say, all these parts should be so

* For military purposes we may take the term "high altitude" as defined by effective vertical range of small-arm fire—in other words, as denoting an altitude of some 5000 ft. or 6000 ft. or more.

§ 12   AIRCRAFT IN WARFARE.

designed that bullets will pass through without doing more than local injury and without serious effect on the strength or flying power of the machine as a whole; in certain cases components will require to be duplicated in order to realise this intention. It is important to understand clearly that any intermediate course is fatal. Either the bullet must be definitely resisted and stopped, or it must be let through with the least possible resistance; it is for the designer to decide in respect of each component which policy he will adopt. The thickness of the armour required will depend very much upon the minimum altitude at which, in the presence of the enemy, it is desired to fly; also upon the particular type of rifle and ammunition brought to bear. There is a great deal of difference in penetrative power, for example, between the round-nosed and pointed bullets used in an otherwise identical cartridge.

If it were not for the consideration of the weight of armour, there is no doubt that an altitude of about 1000 ft. would be found very well suited to most of the ordinary tactical duties of the aeroplane. At such an altitude, however, the thickness of steel plate necessary becomes too serious an item for the present-day machine, even allowing for the very excellent and highly efficient bullet-proof treated steel which is now available; at the altitude in question the minimum thickness that will stop a 0.303 Mark VI. round-nose bullet is 3 mm. ($\frac{1}{8}$ in.), but if attacked by the modern pointed-nose Mauser, nothing short of 5 mm. or 6 mm. is of avail. If we compromise somewhat in the matter of altitude and prescribe 2000 ft. as the minimum height for which protection is to be given, the figures become 2 mm. (about 14 S.W. gauge) for the 0.303 round-nosed bullet, and for the pointed Mauser 3 mm. or slightly over; at present it is not expected that it will pay to armour a machine for the

PLATE IV.

SKELETON OF TYPE B.E.2. Showing position of Tank, Seats, Engine, and Body structure. Illustrates the extent of the vulnerable target presented by an Aeroplane.

DEFENCE FROM GUN-FIRE. § 12

duties in question more heavily; thus we may take 2000 ft. as representing the lower altitude limit of ordinary military flying. Anything less than this will be referred to in the present series of articles as *low-altitude* flying. On this question of armour it cannot be too strongly insisted that anything less than the thickness necessary definitely to stop the projectile is worse than useless; a "mushroomed" bullet, possibly accompanied by a few detached fragments of steel, is infinitely more disagreeable and dangerous than a bullet which has not been upset.

An aeroplane armoured in all its vitals with 3 mm. steel, and otherwise designed on the lines indicated, flying at not less than 2000 ft. altitude, will be extremely difficult to bring down; so much so, that unless its exposed structural members be literally riddled and shattered by rifle and machine-gun, or unless a gun of larger calibre be brought to bear, it will be virtually impossible to effect its capture by gun-fire alone.

CHAPTER IV.
(*September 25th, 1914*).

LOW ALTITUDE FLYING. THE AEROPLANE IN A COMBATANT CAPACITY. THE MACHINE GUN IN THE SERVICE OF THE AERONAUTICAL ARM. THE FUTURE OF THE FIGHTING MACHINE.

§ 13. *Low-Altitude Flying.* Our interest in the subject of low-altitude flying from the military point of view is entirely prospective; there are certain advantages to be derived from low-altitude flying that are not at once apparent; the disadvantages are too obvious to need mention.

It has often been noticed by the writer, and it is probably a matter of common observation, that an aeroplane, however visible it may be with the sky as background, is readily lost to sight and becomes exceedingly difficult to pick out when backed by a hill or a mountain-side. This is the case with a machine finished "bright;"[*] when machines are given protective colouring, as is now customary, the difficulty of detecting their presence when below the sky-line will be far greater. Thus, so long as an aeroplane approaches any position at medium or high altitude, it may be clearly seen at some few miles distance, and measures will be taken to give it an appropriate reception; whereas a machine making its approach at low altitude would frequently be able to take the enemy quite by surprise. Beyond this it has been found that, except for reconnaissance, high altitude is not altogether advantageous.

[*] A term used by boat-builders to denote a varnished boat—not painted.

LOW ALTITUDE FLYING. § 13

A certain amount of harm may be done by bomb-dropping, machine-gun fire, the raining of steel darts, etc.; but an aeroplane at a height cannot take an intimate and decisive part in a fray, as, for an example, cavalry charging, or infantry with the bayonet. It might prove of enormous and overwhelming value if at any critical moment, or at any critical point, it were possible to let loose a few squadrons of aeroplanes each mounting one or more machine guns, to bring short-range concentrated fire to bear, or alternatively to make an attack by the aid of bombs or hand-grenades. The scene that would ensue, for example, on a congested line of retreat would be indescribable: horses thrown into hopeless confusion or stampeded, mechanical transport lorries holed in a dozen or more vital points, water-jackets or radiators damaged, cylinders pierced, etc., gun teams wiped out, infantry decimated; in brief, chaos over endless miles of high road.

§ 14. *Armour for Low-Altitude and Point Blank Range.* The question arises whether it is possible for the aeroplane to fly at a sufficiently low altitude to act effectively in the manner indicated without exposing itself to immediate destruction. The matter is entirely a question of armour; the unarmoured portions of the machine, which derive their immunity from their *transparency* to rifle-fire, are no worse off at point-blank range than at 2000 ft. or 3000 ft. altitude. Taking the altitude as 500 ft. (a reasonable maximum for the effective execution of the duties contemplated), the thickness of armour necessary is approximately $\frac{1}{6}$ in. (4 mm.) for the British service Mark VI. ammunition, or slightly over ¼ in. in the case of the pointed Mauser bullet, the latter thickness representing a weight of 10 lb. per sq. ft. It is evident that the problem of giving complete protection to the motor, pilot, and gunner will become a

§ 14   AIRCRAFT IN WARFARE.

problem of some difficulty; probably in the present state of the constructor's art the protection would need to be somewhat "scamped," and a certain amount of risk admitted. Whatever economies are effected in armour, the main principle must not be lost sight of—*i.e.*, the thickness must not be tampered with; armour too thin for its duty is worse than canvas or brown paper.

Once the altitude has been brought down to 500 ft. —that is to say, if and when it is recognised as advantageous and found possible to utilise such low altitudes in aeroplane tactics—it becomes a question whether it will not be found to pay to "go the whole hog" and fly at the very lowest altitude possible. It may be at once admitted that all the dangers of flying, *qua* flying, will be thereby increased, but danger of the degree in question is a matter of little or no consideration in actual warfare. Briefly, the immediate suggestion is that if low-altitude flying is systematically to be undertaken, it should be conducted *quite* low—dangerously low, according to ordinary standards. At an altitude of 500 ft. an aeroplane still makes a very clear mark against the sky, visible from a considerable distance. By following the contour of the ground, never rising more than 100 ft. or 200 ft., unless to clear an obstacle not otherwise to be avoided, an attack will be made with comparative suddenness, and the machine will be gone out of sight almost before there has been time to bring a gun to bear. Even when under fire it will have a certain tactical advantage in the fact that it will be attacking a *line*[*] parallel to which it is flying—it need never miss its target—whereas it itself offers the worst kind of mark to the enemy, combining small size, high speed, disconcertingly short

[*] In nearly all cases the objective of attack will be a *line* of some kind, thus it may be a convoy or column in retreat, alternatively, if the attack be on an entrenched position or on the attacking force, the line formation is again in evidence, the pilot's instructions in every case would be to fly directly over or parallel to the line to be attacked.

ARMOUR AND ARMAMENT. § 14

range, in addition to which it is, in effect, a disappearing target. If one is tempted to be over-influenced by the obvious danger of such tactics, it is well to recall the exploits carried out as a matter of ordinary experience by cavalry under fire, without the advantage of armoured protection, while presenting a target (man and horse) something like 20 sq. ft. in area, and with a speed contemptibly small in comparison with that of flight. It is only necessary clearly to admit that in this form of fighting we may have to reckon with serious losses of men and machines, not occasional losses, as at present, but rather such as can be expressed as a percentage of the force engaged.

The further reduction of altitude now under discussion means that rifle-fire must be faced literally at muzzle velocity, and corresponding provision made in the thickness of the armour. For the pointed Mauser bullet, representing the maximum requirement of to-day, the thickness of plate needed is scarcely less than $\tfrac{3}{8}$ in., and the weight 13 lb. or 14 lb. per sq. ft. Evidently the question of weight of armour will become a difficulty of a most serious character, and no pretence can be made to give complete protection; the area must be cut down to an absolute minimum.

§ 15. *The Machine-Gun in the Service of the Aeronautical Arm.* Rapidity of fire to the aeronautical gunner is a matter of first importance; the time during which he has the enemy under fire is necessarily brief, and in that time he must do the maximum injury possible; consequently amongst present existing weapons we may regard the machine-gun as without rival.

The degree of accuracy attainable in firing with a machine-gun from an aeroplane depends primarily upon the weapon and the man, as in every other kind of shooting, but in addition the steadiness of the aeroplane

§ 15   AIRCRAFT IN WARFARE.

is an important factor, this being mainly dependent upon the wind and weather. Under favourable conditions an expert shot using the Lewis gun has delivered the whole contents of a magazine (of 47 cartridges capacity) into an area 10 ft. by 60 ft. from an altitude of 600 ft. at a range of 1,000 yards. Making allowance for this expert handling of the weapon, as being superior to the average ability available under service conditions, there can be no doubt as to the deadly efficiency of a gun of the Lewis type as an aeroplane armament. The author has himself witnessed a performance very little inferior to the above in weather that could by no means be considered ideal. Apart from many detail points of merit, the Lewis gun for aeroplane service, has many advantages; firstly, on account of its self-contained magazine, which, by the abolition of the cartridge-belt, etc., permits of the gun being trained freely in any direction from vertically upwards to vertically downwards; secondly, its light weight, which also allows of its use as a shoulder-arm; and, thirdly, the adoption of direct air cooling in place of the usual water-jacket.*

Assuming the proved accuracy of the Lewis gun as the criterion of machine-gun fire, it is evident that an estimate of the effectiveness of low-altitude aeroplane attack becomes little more than a matter of simple arithmetic. We may take, for example, the problem to be that of executing a counter-attack upon infantry, themselves attacking a position in open order, the counter-attack to be delivered against the foremost line, lying prone at two or three paces interval. We are justified in assuming that the magazines will be emptied over an area defined as a belt of 10 ft. or 12 ft. width, in which, therefore, there is one man to approximately 100 sq. ft. of ground under fire. Now the area of target

* Compare Appendix.

FIGHTING AT LOW ALTITUDE.   § 15

offered by a man prone is approximately 5 sq. ft., so that, as an average, one bullet in twenty will find its mark. This represents a man knocked out for every 10 oz. of lead expended, which must be regarded as extremely economical, in view of the fact, that it is usually supposed to take a hundredweight of lead to kill one man, say 30 lb. or 40 lb. for every man put out of action.

§ 16. *Points in Favour of Extreme Low-Altitude.* In any such work as the foregoing, the question of lowness of altitude is of vital importance. Since no attempt to aim at an individual mark is contemplated, there is no disadvantage from the point of view of the gunner in flying quite low. His target may appear as blurred as the side of a railway cutting viewed from the window of an express train, but so long as he "delivers the goods" within the belt of ground intended, his average hits will not be detrimentally affected. If he is shot at by the infantry line he is attacking, or by a supporting line (usually 300 yards, more or less, in the rear), every man attacking him breaks his cover, and becomes a prominent mark for the defending infantry force. Beyond this, the aeroplane carries armour and presents a comparatively small vulnerable target. The advantage of extreme low-altitude flying in the present connection lies in the fact that it is, in effect, a perfect defence against attack by long-range fire. No matter what developments may be made in air-defence artillery —even if means should be found to render an 18-pounder as handy as a sportsman's shot-gun—if the attacking aeroplane fly low enough, the enemy cannot bring long-range fire to bear without bringing his own infantry lines under fire at the same time.

§ 17. *The Future of the Fighting Type of Aeroplane.* A reservation has already been made to the

§ 17   AIRCRAFT IN WARFARE.

effect that low-altitude flying—*i.e.*,, under 2,000 ft.—as affecting the service use of the aeroplane, lies mainly with the future; the design of the machine for this class of work will require the most careful study on the lines already indicated, the essential point being immunity to attack by small-arm fire. In obtaining such immunity sacrifice of some kind will have to be made. Whether it be in the armour-plating of vitals or in the provision of redundant members or material, a great deal of otherwise unnecessary weight must needs be carried which ultimately reduces the carrying power in other directions. This means eventually either a reduction in the speed or a positive all-round increase in the size and weight of the machine. Granted that all initial difficulties be overcome, the advent of the armed and armoured low-altitude machine will initiate a new phase of aeroplane tactics, and one that cannot fail to have a far-reaching effect on the other Arms of the Service. The difficulties of cavalry operations will be increased incalculably; a body of cavalry, unless protected by a covering force of aeroplanes, will find itself continually open to attack, both by short-range machine-gun fire and by bombs and hand-grenades: in addition to this the demoralising effect of numbers of high-powered aeroplanes flying overhead, perhaps within 200 ft. or so, will be by no means a negligible factor. Up to the present the cavalry have been the Arm of greatest mobility, and nearly all cavalry operations on a large scale are fundamentally based upon, and rendered possible by, that fact. Once the aeroplane has taken its place in the actual fighting arena, this condition is definitely a thing of the past, and, so long as daylight lasts at least, any cavalry force not itself accompanied, or supported, by its own aeroplane auxiliary will find its every movement dogged by the hostile aeroplane, and its every operation baulked by counter-attack from above.

PLATE V.

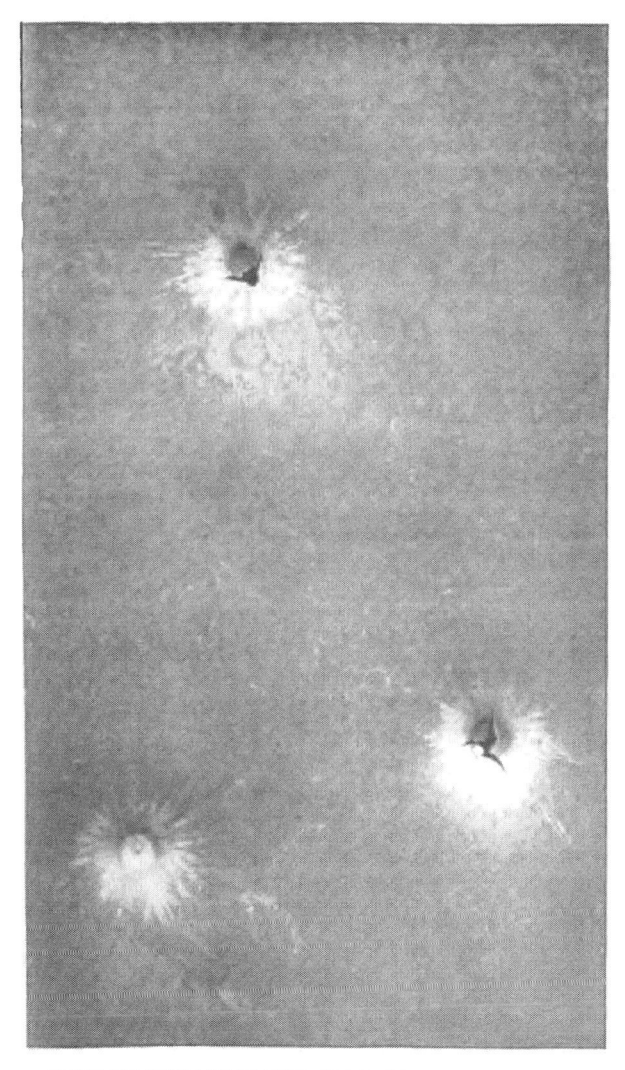

TEST OF "BULLET-PROOF" STEEL PLATE, 3 M.M. THICK.
Range 300 yards. Service Rifle. Mark VI. Ammunition.

AS AFFECTING THE CAVALRY ARM. § 17

Caught in the open, its only defence will be in dispersion over the ·idest possible front or area, otherwise it must take to the woods or whatever other cover is available. Further, it will be impossible for it to undertake a dismounted action, for the led horses (the bugbear of dismounted cavalry) will be either stampeded or destroyed, and its existence as an effective unit will be at an end.

§ 18. *As Affecting the Cavalry Arm.* It must not be supposed, however fully the present anticipations of the development of the aeroplane as a fighting machine may be realised, that the value of cavalry is at an end; this is not the author's view. It is probable that in the early stages of a battle, or of a campaign, the cavalry Arm will cease to play the important *rôle* that at present is, and has hitherto been, assigned to it, and that the pushing out of advance posts and reconnaissance will devolve more and more on the armed and armoured motor-car and aeroplane. However this may be, there will still remain country in which cavalry can be advantageously employed, country in which cover (woods, forests, etc.) is plentiful, where mounted men are secure from aerial observation and attack, and where a mounted force is virtually the only means by aid of which the terrain can be effectively reconnoitred.

Thus, also, in wooded country, in the reconnaissance that accompanies or precedes an army on the march, it would seem probable that the aeroplane and cavalry will be used in conjuction, the more distant work being accomplished by the aeroplane, whose presence would also ensure the protection of the cavalry from hostile aircraft. The detail work, including the holding of bridges and advance positions of importance, also the location of and dealing with any patrols or other bodies of the enemy that may be encountered, will be accomplished by the cavalry. The obvious disadvantage of the

§ 18 AIRCRAFT IN WARFARE.

use of the aeroplane for reconnoitring is that it informs the enemy of the advance or presence of a hostile force. Where this fact is of weight, the protecting flight or squadron of aeroplanes would be best handled as a supporting force, with perhaps one machine at high altitude to maintain contact, the duties of this latter machine being to keep in touch and transmit information to the divisional or army corps command, and to call for the supporting aeroplane force should occasion require. Exactly how the combination of the two Arms (aircraft and cavalry) will be controlled and handled it is impossible, without actual experience, to lay down. The main point is that in the new Arm we have a force altogether transcending the cavalry in mobility and range of observation, and which before long will become an actual fighting force of no mean importance, and these facts cannot fail to be revolutionary in their ultimate influence on the *rôle* and employment of the cavalry Arm.

CHAPTER V.
(October 2nd, 1914).

THE PRINCIPLE OF CONCENTRATION.
THE N-SQUARE LAW.

§ 19. *The Principle of Concentration.* It is necessary at the present juncture to make a digression and to treat of certain fundamental considerations which underlie the whole science and practice of warfare in all its branches. One of the great questions at the root of all strategy is that of *concentration*; the concentration of the whole resources of a belligerent on a single purpose or object, and concurrently the concentration of the main strength of his forces, whether naval or military, at one point in the field of operations. But the principle of concentration is not in itself a strategic principle; it applies with equal effect to purely tactical operations; it is on its material side based upon facts of a purely scientific character. The subject is somewhat befogged by many authors of repute, inasmuch as the two distinct sides—the moral concentration (the narrowing and fixity of purpose) and the material concentration—are both included under one general heading, and one is invited to believe that there is some peculiar virtue in the word *concentration*, like the "blessed word Mesopotamia," whereas the truth is that the word in its two applications refers to two entirely independent conceptions, whose underlying principles have nothing really in common.

The importance of concentration in the material sense is based on certain elementary principles connected

§ 19 AIRCRAFT IN WARFARE.

with the means of attack and defence, and if we are properly to appreciate the value and importance of concentration in this sense, we must not fix our attention too closely upon the bare fact of concentration, but rather upon the underlying principles, and seek a more solid foundation in the study of the controlling factors.

§ 20. *The Conditions of Ancient and Modern Warfare Contrasted.* There is an important difference between the methods of defence of primitive times and those of the present day which may be used to illustrate the point at issue. In olden times, when weapon directly answered weapon, the act of defence was positive and direct, the blow of sword or battleaxe was parried by sword and shield; under modern conditions gun answers gun, the defence from rifle-fire is rifle-fire, and the defence from artillery, artillery. But the defence of modern arms is indirect: tersely, the enemy is prevented from killing you by your killing him first, and the fighting is essentially collective. As a consequence of this difference, the importance of concentration in history has been by no means a constant quantity. Under the old conditions it was not possible by any strategic plan or tactical manœuvre to bring other than approximately equal numbers of men into the actual fighting line; one man would ordinarily find himself opposed to one man. Even were a General to concentrate twice the number of men on any given portion of the field to that of the enemy, the number of men actually wielding their weapons at any given instant (so long as the fighting line was unbroken), was, roughly speaking, the same on both sides. Under present-day conditions all this is changed. With modern long-range weapons—fire-arms, in brief—the concentration of superior numbers gives an immediate superiority in the active combatant ranks, and the numerically inferior force finds itself under a far heavier

THE PRINCIPLE OF CONCENTRATION. § 20

fire, man for man, than it is able to return. The importance of this difference is greater than might casually be supposed, and, since it contains the kernel of the whole question, it will be examined in detail.

In thus contrasting the ancient conditions with the modern, it is not intended to suggest that the advantages of concentration did not, to some extent, exist under the old order of things. For example, when an army broke and fled, undoubtedly any numerical superiority of the victor could be used with telling effect, and, before this, pressure, as distinct from blows, would exercise great influence. Also the bow and arrow and the cross-bow were weapons that possessed in a lesser degree the

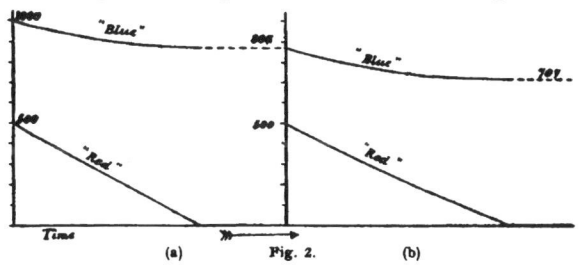

Fig. 2.

properties of fire-arms, inasmuch as they enabled numbers (within limits) to concentrate their attack on the few. As here discussed, the conditions are contrasted in their most accentuated form as extremes for the purpose of illustration.

Taking, first, the ancient conditions where man is opposed to man, then, assuming the combatants to be of equal fighting value, and other conditions equal, clearly, on an average, as many of the "duels" that go to make up the whole fight will go one way as the other, and there will be about equal numbers killed of the forces engaged ; so that if 1,000 men meet 1,000 men, it is of little or no importance whether a "Blue" force of 1,000

§ 20   AIRCRAFT IN WARFARE.

men meet a "Red" force of 1,000 men in a single pitched battle, or whether the whole "Blue" force concentrates on 500 of the "Red" force, and, having annihilated them, turns its attention to the other half; there will, presuming the "Reds" stand their ground to the last, be half the "Blue" force wiped out in the annihilation of the "Red" force* in the first battle, and the second battle will start on terms of equality—*i.e.*, 500 "Blue" against 500 "Red."

§ 21. *Modern Conditions Investigated.* Now let us take the modern conditions. If, again, we assume equal individual fighting value, and the combatants otherwise (as to "cover," etc.) on terms of equality, each man will in a given time score, on an average, a certain number of hits that are effective; consequently, the number of men knocked out per unit time will be directly proportional to the numerical strength of the opposing force. Putting this in mathematical language, and employing symbol b to represent the numerical strength of the "Blue" force, and r for the "Red," we have:—

$$\frac{db}{dt} = - r \times c \quad . \quad . \quad . \quad . \quad (1)$$

and

$$\frac{dr}{dt} = - b \times k \quad . \quad . \quad . \quad . \quad (2)$$

in which t is time and c and k are constants ($c = k$ if the fighting values of the individual units of the force are equal).

The reduction of strength of the two forces may be represented by two conjugate curves following the above equations. In Fig. 2 (*a*) graphs are given representing the case of the "Blue" force 1,000 strong encountering a section of the "Red" force 500 strong, and it will be seen that the "Red" force is wiped out of existence with

* This is not strictly true, since towards the close of the fight the last few men will be attacked by more than their own number. The main principle is, however, untouched.

THE PRINCIPLE OF CONCENTRATION.   § 21

a loss of only about 134 men of the "Blue" force, leaving 866 to meet the remaining 500 of the "Red" force with an easy and decisive victory; this is shown in Fig. 2 (b), the victorious "Blues" having annihilated the whole "Red" force of equal total strength with a loss of only 293 men.

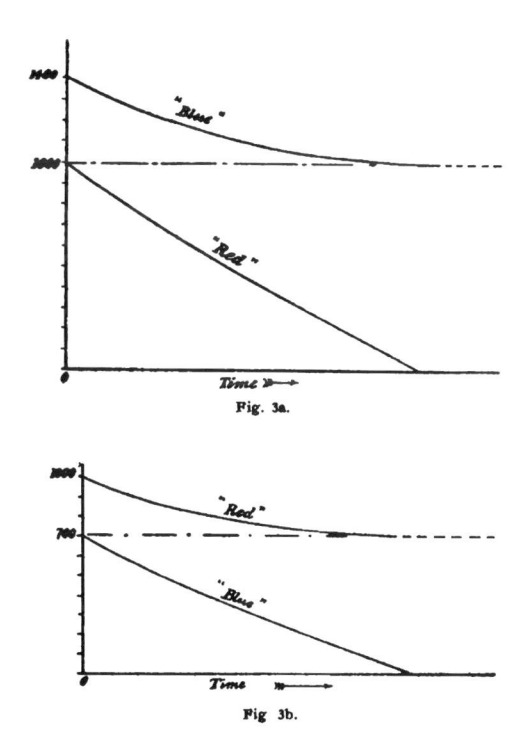

Fig. 3a.

Fig 3b.

In Fig. 3a a case is given in which the "Red" force is inferior to the "Blue" in the relation 1 : √2 say, a "Red" force 1,000 strong meeting a "Blue" force 1,400 strong. Assuming they meet in a single pitched battle fought to a conclusion, the upper line will repre-

§ 21   AIRCRAFT IN WARFARE.

sent the "Blue" force, and it is seen that the "Reds" will be annihilated, the "Blues" losing only 400 men. If, on the other hand, the "Reds" by superior strategy compel the "Blues" to give battle divided—say into two equal armies—then Fig. 3*b*, in the first battle the 700 "Blues" will be annihilated with a loss of only 300 to the "Reds" and in the second battle the two armies will meet on an equal numerical footing, and so we may presume the final battle of the campaign as drawn. In this second case the result of the second battle is presumed from the initial equality of the forces; the curves are not given.

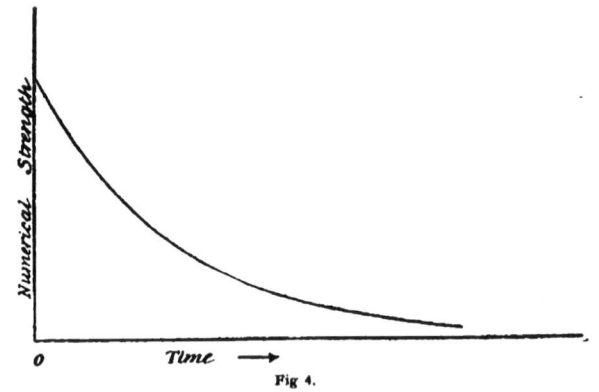

Fig 4.

In the case of equal forces the two conjugate curves become coincident; there is a single curve of logarithmic form, Fig. 4; the battle is prolonged indefinitely. Since the forces actually consist of a finite number of finite units (instead of an infinite number of infinitesimal units), the end of the curve must show discontinuity, and break off abruptly when the last man is reached; the law based on averages evidently does not hold rigidly when the numbers become small. Beyond this, the condition of two equal curves is unstable, and any advantage secured by either side will tend to augment.

THE PRINCIPLE OF CONCENTRATION. § 23

§ 23. *Graph representing Weakness of a Divided Force.* In Fig. 5a, a pair of conjugate curves have been plotted backwards from the vertical datum representing the finish, and an upper graph has been added represent-

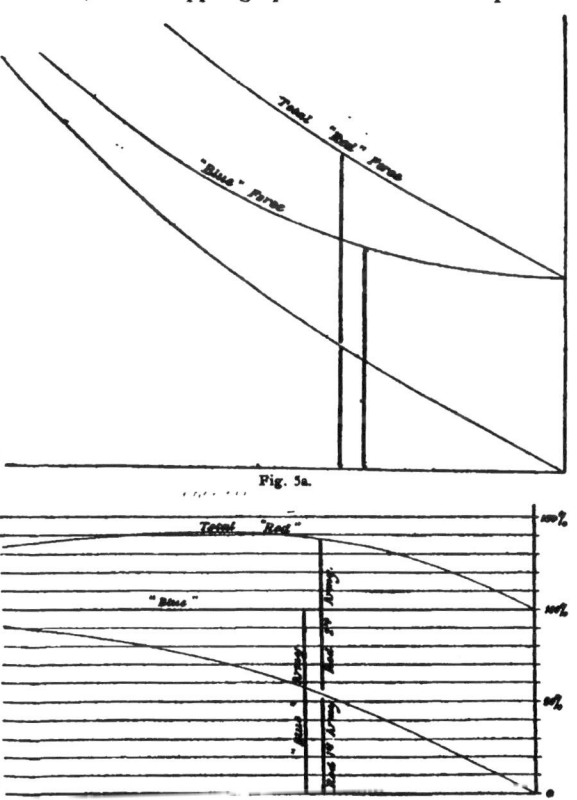

Fig. 5a.

Fig. 5b.

ing the total of the "Red" force, which is equal in strength to the "Blue" force for any ordinate, on the basis that the "Red" force is divided into two portions as given by the intersection of the lower graph. In

§ 23   AIRCRAFT IN WARFARE.

Fig. 5 *b*, this diagram has been reduced to give the same information in terms *per cent.* for a "Blue" force of constant value. Thus in its application Fig. 5 *b* gives the correct percentage increase necessary in the fighting value of, for example, an army or fleet to give equality, on the assumption that political or strategic necessities impose the condition of dividing the said army or fleet into two in the proportions given by the lower graph, the enemy being able to attack either proportion with his full strength. Alternatively, if the constant ($= 100$) be taken to represent a numerical strength that would be deemed sufficient to ensure victory against the enemy, given that both fleets engage in their full strength, then the upper graph gives the numerical superiority needed to be equally sure of victory, in case, from political or other strategic necessity, the fleet has to be divided in the proportions given. In Fig. 5b abscissæ have no quantitative meaning.

§ 24. *Validity of Mathematical Treatment.* There are many who will be inclined to cavil at any mathematical or semi-mathematical treatment of the present subject, on the ground that with so many unknown factors, such as the morale or leadership of the men, the unaccounted merits or demerits of the weapons, and the still more unknown "chances of war," it is ridiculous to pretend to calculate anything. The answer to this is simple: the direct numerical comparison of the forces engaging in conflict or available in the event of war is almost universal. It is a factor always carefully reckoned with by the various military authorities; it is discussed *ad nauseam* in the Press. Yet such direct counting of forces is in itself a tacit acceptance of the applicability of mathematical principles, but confined to a special case. To accept without reserve the mere "counting of the pieces" as of value, and to deny the more extended

CONCENTRATION: THE *N-SQUARE* LAW.   § 24

application of mathematical theory, is as illogical and unintelligent as to accept broadly and indiscriminately the balance and the weighing-machine as instruments of precision, but to decline to permit in the latter case any allowance for the known inequality of leverage.

§ 25. *Fighting Units not of Equal Strength.* In the equations (1) and (2), two constants were given, c and k, which in the plotting of the figures 2 to 5b were taken as equal; the meaning of this is that the fighting strength of the individual units has been assumed equal. This condition is not necessarily fulfilled if the combatants be unequally trained, or of different morale. Neither is it fulfilled if their weapons are of unequal efficiency. The first two of these, together with a host of other factors too numerous to mention, cannot be accounted for in an equation any more than can the quality of wine or steel be estimated from the weight. The question of weapons is, however, eminently suited to theoretical discussion. It is also a matter that (as will be subsequently shown) requires consideration in relation to the main subject of the present articles.

§ 26. *Influence of Efficiency of Weapons.* Any difference in the efficiency of the weapons—for example, the accuracy or rapidity of rifle-fire—may be represented by a disparity in the constants c and k in equations (1) and (2). The case of the rifle or machine-gun is a simple example to take, inasmuch as comparative figures are easily obtained which may be said fairly to represent the fighting efficiency of the weapon. Now numerically equal forces will no longer be forces of equal strength; they will only be of equal strength if, when in combat, their losses result in no change in their numerical proportion. Thus, if a "Blue" force initially 500 strong, using a magazine rifle, attack a "Red" force of 1,000, armed with a single breech-loader, and after a certain

§ 26   AIRCRAFT IN WARFARE.

time the "Blue" are found to have lost 100 against 200 loss by the "Red," the proportions of the forces will have suffered no change, and they may be regarded (due to the superiority of the "Blue" arms) as being of equal strength.

If the condition of equality is given by writing M as representing the efficiency or value of an individual unit of the "Blue" force, and N the same for the "Red," we have:—

Rate of reduction of "Blue" force:—

$$\frac{db}{dt} = - \text{N} r \times \text{constant} \quad . \quad . \quad (3)$$

and "Red,"

$$\frac{dr}{dt} = - \text{M} b \times \text{constant} \quad . \quad . \quad (4)$$

And for the condition of equality,

$$\frac{db}{b\,dt} = \frac{dr}{r\,dt},$$

or

$$\frac{-\text{N} r}{b} = \frac{-\text{M} b}{r},$$

or

$$\text{N} r^2 = \text{M} b^2 \quad . \quad . \quad . \quad (5)$$

In other words, the fighting strengths of the two forces are equal when the *square of the numerical strength multiplied by the fighting value of the individual units are equal.*

§ 27. *The Outcome of the Investigation. The n-square Law.* It is easy to show that this expression (5) may be interpreted more generally; the *fighting strength* of a force may be broadly defined as proportional to *the square of its numerical strength multiplied by the fighting value of its individual units.*

Thus, referring to Fig. 5b, the sum of the squares of the two portions of the "Red" force are for all values equal to the square of the "Blue" force (the latter

THE N-SQUARE LAW: DEMONSTRATION. § 27

plotted as constant); the curve might equally well have been plotted directly to this law as by the process given. A simple proof of the truth of the above law as arising from the differential equations (1) and (2), § 21, is as follows:—

In Fig. 6, let the numerical values of the "blue" and "red" forces be represented by lines b and r as shown; then in an infinitesimally small interval of time the change in b and r will be represented respectively by db and dr of such relative magnitude that $db/dr = r/b$ or,

$$b\ db = r\ dr \qquad (1)$$

If (Fig. 6) we draw the squares on b and r and represent the increments db and dr as small finite incre-

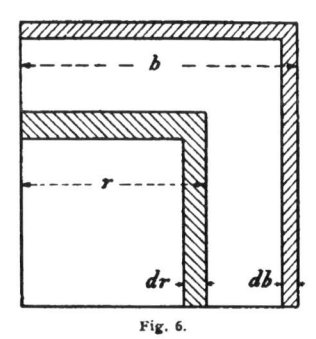

Fig. 6.

ments, we see at once that the *change of area* of b^2 is $2b\ db$ and the *change of area* of r^2 is $2r\ dr$ which according to the foregoing (1), are equal. Therefore the difference between the two squares is constant

$$b^2 - r^2 = \text{constant}.$$

If this constant be represented by a quantity q^2 then $b^2 = r^2 + q^2$ and q represents the numerical value of the remainder of the blue "force" after annihilation

§ 28   AIRCRAFT IN WARFARE.

of the red. Alternatively q represents numerically a second "red" army of the strength necessary in a *separate action* to place the red forces on terms of equality, as in Fig. 5b.

§ 28. *A Numerical Example.* As an example of the above, let us assume an army of 50,000 giving battle in turn to two armies of 40,000 and 30,000 respectively, equally well armed; then the strengths are equal, since $(50,000)^2 = (40,000)^2 + (30,000)^2$. If, on the other hand, the two smaller armies are given time to effect a junction, then the army of 50,000 will be overwhelmed, for the fighting strength of the opposing force, 70,000 is no longer equal, but is in fact nearly twice as great—namely, in the relation of 49 to 25. Superior morale or better tactics or a hundred and one other extraneous causes may intervene in practice to modify the issue, but this does not invalidate the mathematical statement.

§ 29. *Example Involving Weapons of Different Effective Value.* Let us now take an example in which a difference in the fighting value of the unit is a factor. We will assume that, as a matter of experiment, one man employing a machine-gun can punish a target to the same extent in a given time as sixteen riflemen. What is the number of men armed with the machine gun necessary to replace a battalion a thousand strong in the field? Taking the fighting value of a rifleman as unity, let n = the number required. The fighting strength of the battalion is, $(1,000)^2$ or,

$$n = \sqrt{\frac{1,000,000}{16}} = \frac{1,000}{4} = 250$$

or one quarter the number of the opposing force.

This example is instructive; it exhibits at once the utility and weakness of the method. The basic assumption is that the fire of each force is definitely *concentrated*

CONCENTRATION: THE CONDITIONS VARIED. § 29

on the opposing force. Thus the enemy will concentrate on the one machine-gun operator the fire that would otherwise be distributed over four riflemen, and so on an average he will only last for one quarter the time, and at sixteen times the efficiency during his short life he will only be able to do the work of four riflemen in lieu of sixteen, as one might easily have supposed. This is in agreement with the equation. The conditions may be regarded as corresponding to those prevalent in the Boer War, when individual-aimed firing or sniping was the order of the day.

When, on the other hand, the circumstances are such as to preclude the possibility of such concentration, as when searching an area or ridge at long range, or volley firing at a position, or "into the brown," the basic conditions are violated, and the value of the individual machine-gun operator becomes more nearly that of the sixteen riflemen that the power of his weapon represents. The same applies when he is opposed by shrapnel fire or any other weapon which is directed at a position rather than the individual. It is well thus to call attention to the variations in the conditions and the nature of the resulting departure from the conclusions of theory; such variations are far less common in naval than in military warfare; the individual unit—the ship—is always the gunner's mark. When we come to deal with aircraft, we shall find the conditions in this respect more closely resemble those that obtain in the Navy than in the Army; the enemy's aircraft individually rather than collectively is the air-gunner's mark, and the law herein laid down will be applicable.

§ 30. *The Hypothesis Varied.* Apart from its connection with the main subject, the present line of treatment has a certain fascination, and leads to results which, though probably correct, are in some degree

§ 30 AIRCRAFT IN WARFARE.

unexpected. If we modify the initial hypothesis to harmonise with the conditions of long-range fire, and assume the fire concentrated on a certain area known to be held by the enemy, and take this area to be independent of the numerical value of the forces, then, with notation as before, we have—

$$\left. \begin{array}{l} -\dfrac{db}{dt} = b \times N\ r \\ -\dfrac{dr}{dt} = r \times M\ b \end{array} \right\} \times \text{constant.}$$

or

$$M\dfrac{db}{dt} = N\dfrac{dr}{dt}$$

or the rate of loss is independent of the numbers engaged, and is directly as the efficiency of the weapons. Under these conditions the fighting strength of the forces is directly proportional to their numerical strength; there is no direct value in concentration, *qua* concentration, and the advantage of rapid fire is relatively great. Thus in effect the conditions approximate more closely to those of ancient warfare.

§ 31. *An Unexpected Deduction.* Evidently it is the business of a numerically superior force to come to close quarters, or, at least, to get within decisive range as rapidly as possible, in order that the concentration may tell to advantage. As an extreme case, let us imagine a " Blue " force of 100 men armed with the machine gun opposed by a " Red " 1,200 men armed with the ordinary service rifle. Our first assumption will be that both forces are spread over a front of given length and at long range. Then the " Red " force will lose 16 men to the " Blue " force loss of one, and, if the combat is continued under these conditions, the " Reds" must lose. If, however, the "Reds" advance, and get within short range, where each man and gunner is an

CONCENTRATION: EXAMPLES FROM HISTORY. § 31

individual mark, the tables are turned, the previous equation and conditions apply, and, even if "Reds" lose half their effective in gaining the new position, with 600 men remaining they are masters of the situation; their strength is $600^2 \times 1$ against the "Blue" $100^2 \times 16$. It is certainly a not altogether expected result that, in the case of fire so deadly as the modern machine-gun, circumstances may arise that render it imperative, and at all costs, to come to close range.

§ 32. *Examples from History.* It is at least agreed by all authorities that on the field of battle concentration is a matter of the most vital importance; in fact, it is admitted to be one of the controlling factors both in the strategy and tactics of modern warfare. It is aptly illustrated by the important results that have been obtained in some of the great battles of history by the attacking of opposing forces before concentration has been effected. A classic example is that of the defeat by Napoleon, in his Italian campaign, of the Austrians near Verona, where he dealt with the two Austrian armies in detail before they had been able to effect a junction, or even to act in concert. Again, the same principle is exemplified in the oft-quoted case of the defeat of Jourdan and Moreau on the Danube by the Archduke Charles in 1796. It is evident that the conditions in the broad field of military operations correspond in kind, if not in degree, to the earlier hypothesis, and that the law deduced therefrom, that the fighting strength of a force can be represented by the square of its numerical strength, does, in its essence, represent an important truth.

CHAPTER VI.
(October 9th, 1914)

THE N-SQUARE LAW IN ITS APPLICATION.

§ 33. *The n-square Law in its Application to a Heterogeneous Force.* In the preceding article it was demonstrated that under the conditions of modern warfare the fighting strength of a force, so far as it depends upon its numerical strength, is best represented or measured by the square of the number of units. In land operations these units may be the actual men engaged, or in an artillery duel the gun battery may be the unit; in a naval battle the number of units will be the number of capital ships, or in an action between aeroplanes the number of machines. In all cases where the individual fighting strength of the component units may be different it has been shown that if a numerical fighting value can be assigned to these units, the fighting strength of the whole force is as the square of the number multiplied by their individual strength. Where the component units differ among themselves, as in the case of a fleet that is not homogeneous, the measure of the total of fighting strength of a force will be *the square of the sum of the square roots of the strengths of its individual units.*

§ 34. *Graphic Representation.* Before attempting to apply the foregoing, either as touching the conduct of aerial warfare or the equipment of the fighting aeroplane, it is of interest to examine a few special cases and applications in other directions and to discuss certain possible limitations. A convenient graphic form in which the

THE N-SQUARE LAW IN ITS APPLICATION. § 34

operation of the *n-square* law can be presented is given in Fig. 7 ; here the strengths of a number of separate armies or forces successively mobilised and brought into action are represented numerically by the lines *a, b, c, d, e*, and the aggregate fighting strengths of these armies are given by the lengths of the lines A, B, C, D, E, each being the hypotenuse of a right-angle triangle, as indicated Thus two forces or armies *a* and *b*, if acting separately (in point of time), have only the fighting

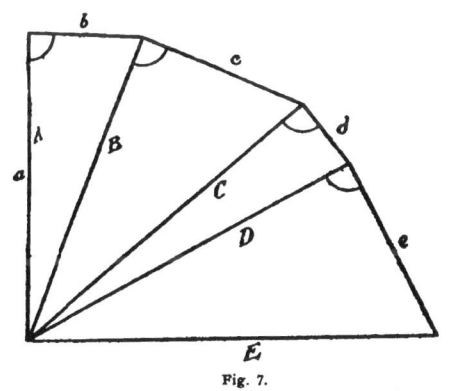

Fig. 7.

strength of a single force or army represented numerically by the line B. Again, the three separate forces, *a, b*, and *c*, could be met on equal terms in three successive battles by a single army of the numerical strength C, and so on.

§ 35. *Special or Extreme Case.* From the diagram given in Fig. 7 arises a special case that at first sight may look like a *reductio ad absurdum*, but which, correctly interpreted, is actually a confirmation of the *n-square* law. Referring to Fig. 7, let us take it that the initial force (army or fleet), is of some definite finite magnitude, but that the later arrivals *b, c, d*, etc., be very small and numerous detachments—so small, in fact, as to

§ 35   AIRCRAFT IN WARFARE.

be reasonably represented to the scale of the diagram as infinitesimal quantities. Then the lines b, c, d, e, f, etc., describe a polygonal figure approximating to a circle which in the limit becomes a circle, whose radius is represented by the original force a, Fig. 8. Here we have graphically represented the result that the fighting value of the added forces, no matter what their numerical aggregate (represented in Fig. 8 by the circumferential

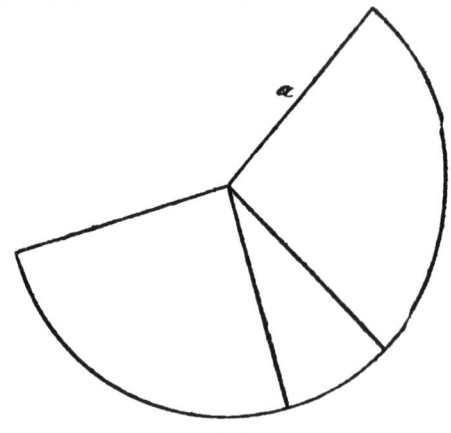

Fig. 8.

line), is zero. The correct interpretation of this is that in the open a small force attacking, or attacked by one of overwhelming magnitude is wiped out of existence without being able to exact a toll even comparable to its own numerical value; it is necessary to say *in the open*, since, under other circumstances, the larger force is unable to bring its weapons to bear, and this is an essential portion of the basic hypothesis. In the limiting case when the disparity of force is extreme, the capacity of the lesser force to effect anything at all becomes negligible. There is nothing improbable in this conclusion, but it manifestly does not apply to the case of a small force concealed or

THE N-SQUARE LAW IN NAVAL WARFARE. § 35

"dug in," since the hypothesis is infringed. Put bluntly, the condition represented in Fig. 8 illustrates the complete impotence of small forces in the presence of one of overwhelming power. Once more we are led to contrast the ancient conditions, under which the weapons of a large army could not be brought to bear, with modern conditions, where it is physically possible for the weapons of ten thousand to be concentrated on one. Macaulay's lines

> "In yon strait path a thousand
> May well be stopped by three,"

belong intrinsically to the methods and conditions of the past.

§ 36. *The N-square Law in Naval Warfare.* We have already seen that the *n-square* law applies broadly, if imperfectly, to military operations; on land however, there sometimes exist special conditions and a multitude of factors extraneous to the hypothesis whereby its operation may be suspended or masked. In the case of naval warfare, however, the conditions more strictly conform to our basic assumptions, and there are comparatively few disturbing factors. Thus, when battle fleet meets battle fleet, there is no advantage to the defender analogous to that secured by the entrenchment of infantry. Again, from the time of opening fire, the individual ship is the mark of the gunner, and there is no phase of the battle or range at which areas are searched in a general way. In a naval battle every shot fired is aimed or directed at some definite one of the enemy's ships; there is no firing on the mass or "into the brown." Under the old conditions of the sailing-ship and cannon of some 1,000 or 1,200 yards maximum effective range, advantage could be taken of concentration within limits; and an examination of the latter 18th century tactics makes it apparent that with any ordinary

§ 36   AIRCRAFT IN WARFARE.

disparity of numbers (probably in no case exceeding 2 to 1) the effect of concentration must have been not far from that indicated by theory. But to whatever extent this was the case, it is certain that with a battle-fleet action at the present day the conditions are still more favourable to the weight of numbers, since with the modern battle range—some 4 to 5 miles—there is virtually no limit to the degree of concentration of fire. Further than this, there is in modern naval warfare practically no chance of coming to close qnarters in ship-to-ship combats, as in the old days.

Thus the conditions are to-day almost ideal from the point of view of theoretical treatment. A numerical superiority of ships of individually equal strength will mean definitely that the inferior fleet at the outset has to face the full fire of the superior, and as the battle proceeds and the smaller fleet is knocked to pieces, the initial disparity will become worse and worse, and the fire to which it is subjected more and more concentrated. These are precisely the conditions taken as the basis of the investigation from which the *n-square* law has been derived. The same observations will probably be found to apply to aerial warfare when air fleets engage in conflict, more especially so in view of the fact that aeroplane can attack aeroplane in three dimensions of space instead of being limited to two, as is the case with the battleship. This will mean that even with weapons of moderate range the degree of fire concentration possible will be very great. By attacking from above and below, as well as from all points of the compass, there is, within reason, no limit to the number of machines which can be brought to bear on a given small force of the enemy, and so a numerically superior fleet will be able to reap every ounce ot advantage from its numbers.

§ 37. *Individual value of Ships or Units.* The factor the most difficult to assess in the evaluation of a fleet as a fighting machine is (apart from the *personnel*) the individual value of its units, when these vary amongst themselves. There is no possibility of entirely obviating this difficulty, since the fighting value of any given ship depends not only upon its gun armament, but also upon its protective armour. One ship may be stronger than another at some one range, and weaker at some longer or shorter range, so that the question of fleet strength can never be reduced quite to a matter of simple arithmetic, nor the design of the battleship to an exact science. In practice the drawing up of a naval programme resolves itself, in great part at least, into the answering of the prospective enemy's programme type by type and ship by ship. It is, however, generally accepted that so long as we are confining our attention to the main battle fleets, and so are dealing with ships of closely comparable gun calibre and range, and armour of approximately equivalent weight, the fighting value of the individual ship may be gauged by the weight of its "broadside," or more accurately, taking into account the speed with which the different guns can be served, by the weight of shot that can be thrown per minute. Another basis, and one that perhaps affords a fairer comparison, is to give the figure for the *energy per minute* for broadside fire, which represents, if we like so to express it, the horsepower of the ship as a fighting machine. Similar means of comparison will probably be found applicable to the fighting aeroplane, though it may be that the *downward fire* capacity will be regarded as of vital importance rather than the broadside fire as pertaining to the battleship.

§ 38. *Applications of the n-square Law.* The *n-square* law tells us at once the price or penalty that must be paid if elementary principles are outraged by the

§ 38   AIRCRAFT IN WARFARE.

division of our battle fleet* into two or more isolated detachments. In this respect our present diposition—a single battle fleet or "Grand" fleet—is far more economical and strategically preferable as a defensive power to the old-time distribution of the Channel Fleet, Mediterranean Fleet, etc. If it had been really necessary, for any political or geographical reason, to maintain two separate battle fleets at such distance asunder as to preclude their immediate concentration in case of attack, the cost to the country would have been enormously

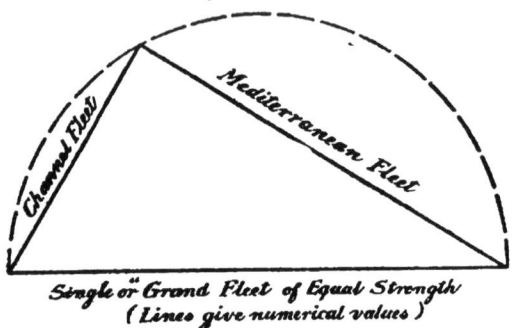

Single or Grand Fleet of Equal Strength
(Lines give numerical values)
Fig. 9

increased. In the case, for example, of our total battle fleet being separated into two equal parts, forming separate fleets or squadrons, the increase would require to be fixed at approximately 40 per cent.—that is to say, in the relation of 1 to $\sqrt{2}$; more generally the solution is given by a right-angled triangle, as in Fig. 9. It must not be forgotten that, even with this enormous increase, the security will not be so great as appears on paper, for the enemy's fleet, having met and defeated one section of our fleet, may succeed in falling back on his base for repair and refit, and emerge later with the advantage of strength in his favour. Also one must not

* Capital ships.—Dreadnoughts and Super-Dreadnoughts.

CONCERNING NAVAL STRATEGY & TACTICS. § 38

overlook the demoralizing effect on the *personnel* of the fleet first to go into action, of the knowledge that they are hopelessly outnumbered and already beaten on paper —that they are, in fact, regarded by their King and country as "cannon fodder." Further than this, presuming two successive fleet actions and the enemy finally beaten, the cost of victory in men and *matériel* will be greater in the case of the divided fleet than in the case of a single fleet of equal total fighting strength, in the proportion of the total numbers engaged—that is to say, in Fig. 9, in the proportion that the two sides of the right-angled triangle are greater than the hypotenuse.

In brief, however potent political or geographical influences or reasons may be, it is questionable whether *under any circumstances* it can be considered sound strategy to divide the main battle fleet on which the defence of a country depends. This is to-day the accepted view of every naval strategist of repute, and is the basis of the present distribution of Great Britain's naval forces.

§ 39. *Fire Concentration the Basis of Naval Tactics.* The question of fire concentration is again found to be paramount when we turn to the consideration and study of naval tactics. It is worthy of note that the recognition of the value of any definite tactical scheme does not seem to have been universal until quite the latter end of the 18th century. It is even said that the French Admiral Suffren, about the year 1780, went so far as to attribute the reverses suffered by the French at sea to "the introduction of tactics" which he stigmatised as "the veil of timidity;"[*] the probability is that the then existing standard of seamanship in the French Navy was so low that anything beyond the simplest of manœuvres led to confusion, not unattended by danger. The subject,

[*] Mahan, "Sea Power," page 425.

§ 39　AIRCRAFT IN WARFARE.

however, was, about that date, receiving considerable attention. A writer, Clerk, about 1780, pointed out that in meeting the attack of the English the French had adopted a system of defence consisting of a kind of running fight, in which, initially taking the "lee gage," they would await the English attack in line ahead, and having delivered their broadsides on the leading English ships (advancing usually in line abreast), they would bear away to leeward and take up position, once more waiting for the renewal of the attack, when the same process was repeated.[*] By these tactics the French obtained a concentration of fire on a small portion of the English fleet, and so were able to inflict severe punishment with little injury to themselves.[†] Here we see the beginnings of sound tactical method adapted to the needs of defence.

Up to the date in question there appears to have been no studied attempt to found a scheme of attack on the basis of concentration; the old order was to give battle in parallel columns or lines, ship to ship, the excess of ships, if either force were numerically superior, being doubled on the rear ships of the enemy. It was not till the "Battle of the Saints," in 1782, that a change took place; Rodney (by accident or intention) broke away from tradition, and cutting through the lines of the enemy, was able to concentrate on his centre and rear, achieving thereby a decisive victory.

§ 40. *British Naval Tactics in 1805. The Nelson "Touch."* The accident or experiment of 1782 had evidently become the established tactics of the British in the course of the twenty years which followed, for not only do we find the method in question carefully laid down in the plan of attack given in the Memorandum issued by

[*] Compare Mahan, "Sea Power," page 162.
[†] Incidentally, also, the scheme in question had the advantage of subjecting the English to a raking fire from the French broadsides before they were themselves able to bring their own broadside fire to bear.

NELSON'S TACTICAL SCHEME. § 40

Nelson just prior to the Battle of Trafalgar in 1805, but the French Admiral Villeneuve* confidently asserted in a note issued to his staff in anticipation of the battle that :— " The British Fleet will not be formed in a line-of-battle parallel to the combined fleet according to the usage of former days. Nelson, assuming him to be, as represented, really in command, will seek to break our line, envelop our rear, and overpower with groups of his ships as many as he can isolate and cut off." Here we have a concise statement of a definite tactical scheme based on a clear understanding of the advantages of fire concentration.

It will be understood by those acquainted with the sailing-ship of the period that the van could only turn to come to the assistance of those in the rear at the cost of a considerable interval of time, especially if the van should happen to be to leeward of the centre and rear. The time taken to "wear ship," or in light winds to "go about" (often only to be effected by manning the boats and rowing to assist the manœuvre), was by no means an inconsiderable item. Thus it would not uncommonly be a matter of some hours before the leading ships could be brought within decisive range, and take an active part in the fray.

§ 41. *Nelson's Memorandum and Tactical Scheme.* In order further to embarass the enemy's van, and more effectively to prevent it from coming into action, it became part of the scheme of attack that a few ships, a comparatively insignificant force, should be told off to intercept and engage as many of the leading ships as possible; in brief, to fight an independent action on a small scale; we may say admittedly a losing action. In this connection Nelson's memorandum of October 9 is illuminating. Nelson assumed for the purpose of framing

* "The Enemy at Trafalgar," Ed. Fraser; Hodder and Stoughton, page 54.

§ 41   AIRCRAFT IN WARFARE.

his plan of attack that his own force would consist of forty sail of the line, against forty-six of the combined (French and Spanish) fleet. These numbers are considerably greater, as things turned out, than those ultimately engaged; but we are here dealing with the memorandum, and not with the actual battle. The British Fleet was to form in two main columns, comprising sixteen sail of the line each, and a smaller column

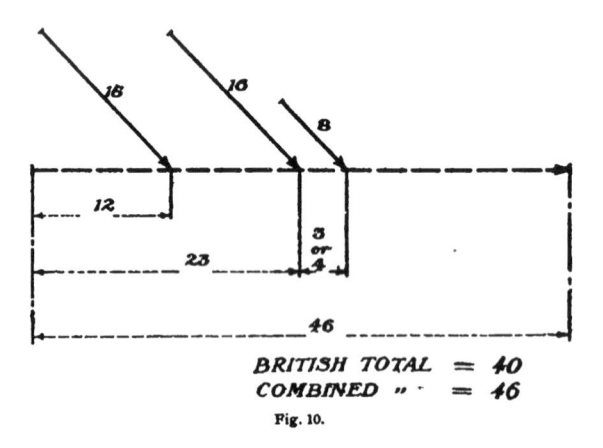

BRITISH TOTAL = 40
COMBINED ,, ˮ = 46

Fig. 10.

of eight ships only. The plan of attack prescribed in the event of the enemy being found in line ahead was briefly as follows:—One of the main columns was to cut the enemy's line about the centre, the other to break through about twelve ships from the rear, the smaller column being ordered to engage the rear of the enemy's van three or four ships ahead of the centre, and to frustrate, as far as possible, every effort the van might make to come to the succour of the threatened centre or rear. Its object, in short, was to prevent the van of the combined fleet from taking part in the main action. The plan is shown diagrammatically in Fig. 10.

THE N-SQUARE LAW AT TRAFALGAR. § 42

§ 42. Nelson's Tactical Scheme Analysed. An examination of the numerical values resulting from the foregoing disposition is instructive. The force with which Nelson planned to envelop the half—*i.e.*, 23 ships —of the combined fleet amounted to 32 ships in all; this according to the n^2 law would give him a superiority of fighting strength of almost exactly two to one,[*] and would mean that if subsequently he had to meet the other half of the combined fleet, without allowing for any injury done by the special eight-ship column, he would have been able to do so on terms of equality. The fact that the van of the combined fleet would most certainly be in some degree crippled by its previous encounter is an indication and measure of the positive advantage of strength provided by the tactical scheme. Dealing with the position arithmetically, we have :—

Strength of British (in arbitrary n^2 units),
$$32^2 + 8^2 = 1088$$
And combined fleet,
$$23^2 + 23^2 = \underline{1058}$$
British advantage 30

Or, the numerical equivalent of the remains of the British Fleet (assuming the action fought to the last gasp), $= \sqrt{30}$ or $5\frac{1}{2}$ ships.

If for the purpose of comparison we suppose the total forces had engaged under the conditions described by Villeneuve as " the usage of former days," we have :—

Strength of combined fleet, 46^2 .... $= 2116$
  ,,   British   ,, 40^2 .... $= \underline{1600}$

Balance in favour of enemy   516

Or, the equivalent numerical value of the remainder of the combined fleet, assuming complete annihilation of the British, $= \sqrt{516} = 23$ ships approximately.

[*] $23 \times \sqrt{2} = 32.5$

§ 42 AIRCRAFT IN WARFARE.

Thus we are led to appreciate the commanding importance of a correct tactical scheme. If in the actual battle the old-time method of attack had been adopted, it is extremely doubtful whether the superior seamanship and gunnery of the British could have averted defeat. The actual forces on the day were 27 British sail of the line against the combined fleet numbering 33, a rather less favourable ratio than assumed in the Memorandum. In the battle, as it took place, the British attacked in two columns instead of three, as laid down in the Memorandum; but the scheme of concentration followed the original idea. The fact that the wind was of the lightest was alone sufficient to determine the exclusion of the enemy's van from the action. However, as a study the Memorandum is far more important than the actual event, and in the foregoing analysis it is truly remarkable to find, firstly, the definite statement of the cutting the enemy into two *equal* parts—according to the *n-square* law the exact proportion corresponding to the reduction of his total effective strength to a minimum; and, secondly, the selection of a proportion, the nearest whole-number equivalent to the $\sqrt{2}$ ratio of theory, required to give a fighting strength equal to tackling the two halves of the enemy on level terms, and the detachment of the remainder, the column of eight sail, to weaken and impede the leading half of the enemy's fleet to guarantee the success of the main idea. If, as might fairly be assumed, the foregoing is more than a coincidence,[*] it suggests itself that Nelson, if not actually acquainted with the *n-square* law, must have had some equivalent basis on which to figure his tactical values.

---

[*] Although we may take it to be a case in which the dictates of experience resulted in a disposition now confirmed by theory, the agreement is remarkable.

CHAPTER VII.
(October 16th, 1914).

ATTACK BY AEROPLANE ON AEROPLANE. THE FIGHTING MACHINE AND ITS ARMAMENT.

§ 43. *Attack by Aeroplane on Aeroplane.* In the present war the services of the Flying Corps have, in the main, been confined to scouting and reconnaissance in its various forms, the amount of work which has been done in this direction being very great; according to present reports, a mileage equivalent to many circuits of the globe has already been covered. So far the casualties have been slight, and the actual risk and danger are considered less than in the other combatant branches of the Service. The meaning of this evidently is that the methods of attack on aircraft have not kept pace with the development of the craft themselves. Considering the importance, from the enemy's point of view, of interfering with the operations of our aircraft (for from a modern standpoint to annihilate the aircraft of an enemy is virtually to deprive him of his power of vision), it is quite certain that the present conditions cannot last, and means will assuredly be found before the next great war, if not during the continance of the present war, by which the attack of aeroplane on aeroplane will be rendered far more deadly than at present, and the air forces of both combatants will be more highly organised to this end than is the case to-day.

It has already been remarked that attack on so swift and, in effect, on so small a moving target as an aeroplane

§ 43   AIRCRAFT IN WARFARE.

is by no means an easy problem. We have already discussed the difficulties of attack from the ground, and it now remains to examine the problem of attack by air— *i.e.*, attack by aeroplane on aeroplane.

At one time the author was disposed to be somewhat sceptical as to the possibility, or rather the general feasibility, of such a mode of attack. It seemed as though aeronauts might spend hours manœuvring and firing, and between them blow away hundreds of pounds weight of ammunition without any decisive result. On closer consideration, however, it would appear that, provided one machine can, either by greater speed, or power of manœuvre, force the other to close quarters, there are conditions (as when both machines are moving in the same direction), under which gun-fire (especially machine-gun fire) could be brought to bear with conclusive effect. We have already been regaled from time to time by the Press with florid descriptions of aeroplane fights in which pilots or observers were said to blaze away at each other with automatic pistols, and it has frequently been stated that the enemy has been brought down by this means. After careful inquiries in quarters believed to be well informed, the author is disposed to discredit these stories. Doubtless attempts have been made by one pilot, or aeronaut, on another by rifle and pistol fire, but there is not, so far as the author has been able to ascertain, any definite record of casualties resulting.*

§ 44. *The Fighting Machine as a Separate Type.* It is at present uncertain whether the scouting or reconnaissance machine will itself in the future be called upon to fight : the view has already been expressed in these articles that the long-distance machine or strategic scout should not in any sense be considered as a fighter, its speed and

* Quite true at the date of the original article ; the Press accounts were in no sense reliable. *Intelligent anticipation* is the usual designation.

PLATE VI.

R.A.F. TYPE F.E.2. Designed to carry gun weight 300 lbs. Wings interchangeable with B.E.2. Speed: Max. 69 m/h. Climb 1,000 ft. in 3½ minutes. *Designed and built in 1913.*

THE FIGHTING MACHINE. § 44

power of rapidly putting on altitude alone form its natural and most appropriate means of defence. The tactical scout is not in the same position; its duties are of such a character that if it be driven by hostile aircraft away from its place of operation, it has for the time being ceased to fulfil its mission, and so either it must always operate with a protective force of fighting machines within call, or it must itself be armed, and be rendered capable of putting up a fight. In any case the tactical scout or machine for local reconnaissance will require to be furnished, to some extent at least, with both offensive and defensive armament. But it is by no means clear that it will require to be armed more heavily than may be sufficient to hold its own with the aircraft of the enemy engaged on similar duty, or than required to enable it to perform the minor acts of aggression against the enemy's land forces that fall to its lot.

Evidently it can be only a matter of time before the specialised fighting-machine is called into being. We may admit that the first and more immediate step will be to render the tactical reconnaissance type capable of taking the offensive, so that it may establish its ascendency over the similar craft of the enemy. But the struggle for supremacy in the air which must then ensue will call imperatively for something more powerful and efficient, a specialised and heavily-armed fighting-machine in fact. It is this type, the fighting machine of the future, that the author proposes to make the subject of present study, discussing primarily the factors upon which its armament and its usage, or tactical employment, depend. It may be taken that for the period during which the tactical scout is playing the double *rôle* of reconnaissance-machine and fighting-machine the main general considerations will apply.

§ 45 AIRCRAFT IN WARFARE.

§ 45. *The Question of Armament; Treaty Restrictions.* In the specification of a fighting type of aeroplane the first and foremost consideration is its means of attack. These fall into two broadly distinct categories: fire-arms, chief amongst which for the purpose in question is the machine-gun or mitrailleuse; and gravitational weapons, including bombs, hand-grenades, steel darts, etc. ; the latter being mainly useful when attacking a terrestrial objective. Except when dealing with a dirigible or airship, gravitational weapons are but ill suited to the conditions of attack on aircraft. Light artillery may certainly be mounted on an aeroplane, but only the very smallest calibre—namely, the " 1-pounder "—can be considered suitable for machines such as are built at the present day; even the mounting of a gun of this size is a matter of great difficulty. The only advantage obtained by the employment of a weapon of this character is in the fact that it is permissible to throw shell, high-explosive or otherwise, the use of which for smaller sizes of projectiles is prohibited by treaty obligation. Any explosive projectile of less than 1 lb. weight (more exactly 400 grammes, or 14 oz., about) is banned by the Declaration of St. Petersburg,* of 1868; the paragraph with which we are concerned reads:—" The contracting parties engage mutually to renounce in case of war amongst themselves the employment by their military or naval troops, of any projectile of a weight below 400 grammes which is either explosive or charged with fulminating or inflammable substances." This is reaffirmed in the text of an abortive declaration of the Brussels Conference of 1874, Article 13 (e): "The use of arms, projectiles, or material which may cause unnecessary suffering, as well as the use of

---

* The signatories to this Declaration include representatives of the following — Great Britain, Austria and Hungary, Belgium, Denmark, France, Greece, Italy, Netherlands, Persia, Portugal, Russia, Sweden and Norway, Switzerland, and Turkey. The German Confederation and semi-independent States were also signatories; but in view of the doctrines of modern Germany as touching the value of international treaties, her signature cannot be taken as meaning anything.

ARMAMENT: TREATY RESTRICTIONS. § 45

the projectiles prohibited by the Declaration of St. Petersburg in 1868." In the Hague Conference of 1899, Article 23 (*e*), it is prohibited "To employ arms, projectiles, or material of a nature to cause superfluous injury." Also Article 60, Declaration ii.:—"The contracting parties agree to abstain from the use of bullets that expand or flatten easily in the human body, such as bullets with a hard envelope which does not entirely cover the core, or is pierced with incisions." In view of the fact that the Brussels Conference of 1874 was sterile, and that the Hague Declaration ii., Article 60, was not subscribed to by the British representative, the Declaration of St. Petersburg with its 14 oz. minimum for explosive projectiles is the only *definite* statement by which we are bound. However, the restriction as to the employment of dum-dum or expanding bullets appears to have received our tacit acquiescence, at least in so far as concerns warfare with other civilised States. There is also the rather indefinite statement of the Hague Conference of 1899, to which we have subscribed, to the effect that we shall not employ arms, projectiles, or material of a nature to cause superfluous injury. The subject of these restrictions will be taken up again in a later chapter; it is here sufficient to point to their existence, and to the fact that they considerably hamper and restrict the development of aircraft and counter-aircraft armament. There seems to be no proper reason why we should be compelled to use some hundreds of unsuitable projectiles, specially designed to afford the least possible injury to the struts, spars, etc., through which they pass, when a comparatively few expanding or explosive bullets would do vastly more injury, and result in a machine being incapacitated both in less time and at less expense. It cannot be supposed that if one of the nations at present at war were to inaugurate the practice of utilising,

§ 45 AIRCRAFT IN WARFARE.

against aircraft, projectiles infringing the Declaration of St. Petersburg, there would be any great wave of indignation created in the world at large. If, for example, we were to find our aircraft being knocked about by such means, we need not imagine that we should receive much compensation in the way of international sympathy. The author is not for a moment suggesting that we should initiate any departure from the accepted usage of warfare in this respect; he is rather questioning the ethics of a procedure by which a country, whose obligations and responsibilities are as wide and as heavy as those of Great Britain, and whose traditions and the force of public opinion make solemn contracts binding, should become a signatory to agreements which are always liable to be (and sometimes are) signed by the other party with his tongue in his cheek. At the best the signing of restrictive agreements relating to the conduct of war may at some time after turn out to be no more or less than the drawing of a cheque on another's banking account—a cheque that will be honoured in another man's blood.

§ 46. *The One-Pounder as an Aeroplane Gun.* For the time being we will take the restrictions imposed by international agreement as though they were restrictions imposed by Nature, and accept the fact that for the throwing of explosive or inflammable projectiles the "one-pounder" is the smallest gun available. At present this offers considerable difficulty in the case of an aeroplane. In order to throw a 14 oz. projectile with a muzzle velocity of 1,700 ft.-sec., the weight of gun and its mountings, including suitable recoil mechanism, could not be much less than 1 cwt., and with 100 rounds of ammunition the total would be about 2½ cwt. Now this weight alone cannot be considered in any sense prohibitive; in fact, it is no more than most of the existing machines in service would be able to carry. But the

THE ONE-POUNDER AS AN AEROPLANE GUN. § 46

difficulties of design are not confined to the weight problem; the gun would have a length from muzzle to breech of 4 ft. or 5 ft., in addition to about 1 ft. representing its movement on recoil, as permitted by the buffer mechanism. To accommodate such a weapon, with reasonable freedom in elevation and traverse, would almost require that the gun be designed first, and that the aeroplane be *designed round it*. The difficulties can only be properly appreciated by taking a drawing-board and paper and endeavouring to find a practicable solution. Beyond the initial difficulties of the problem, it is very doubtful whether it will be found to pay to attack a hostile aeroplane with so large a shell as required by the 14 oz. limit. If a thoroughly sensitive fuse were available, so that the shell would explode on impact with canvas, matters would wear a different aspect, for the wing spread of an aeroplane presents a target of respectable size. However, as things stand, with a total of only about 100 rounds at command, and so small and elusive a target, it is doubtful whether, save under very exceptional circumstances, it would pay to throw away ammunition in pursuit. If the problem be that of attacking a dirigible, it may be considered more hopeful; there is actually more to hit, besides the fact that the aeroplane, in the matter of speed, has the balloon always at a disadvantage; here again the importance of a sensitive impact fuse is paramount.

The necessity for being sparing in the use of ammunition must not be taken to mean (as sometimes represented) that there is no advantage in rapidity of fire, but rather the contrary, and any aeroplane armament gun must be essentially a quick-firer, if not actually automatic or semi-automatic; it is of vital importance that when the opportunity does occur, the utmost use should be made of it. When an aeroplane is within

§ 46   AIRCRAFT IN WARFARE.

decisive range of its prey, it must be presumed that it is itself also under fire, and all the conditions discussed in the foregoing articles apply. If a machine, type A, has four times the rate of fire of another machine, type B, the machine A, *so long as its ammunition holds out*, is worth as much as two machines of the type B. In the case of the one-pounder now under discussion, this condition of the exhaustion of the ammunition is just the weak point which renders it doubtful whether under existing circumstances it is worth while seriously to consider the mounting of such a weapon. It is doubtful, also, whether a fully automatic gun of this calibre is admissible with aeroplanes of present-day dimensions, on account of the mean recoil reaction. This is approximately 1 lb. per shot per minute, or at a rate of 100 per minute, 100 lb.; a quantity that would still further hamper the designer in the arrangement of his gun position.

§ 47. *The Machine-Gun; Importance of Rapid Fire.* For the time being there is no doubt that the ordinary machine-gun is the most serviceable and effective weapon available. Taking, for example, the Lewis gun with its self-contained magazine, the weight of the weapon mounted in place is under 30 lb., and the service ammunition runs 17 to the pound. Assuming, as before, 2½ cwt. as the available total, and taking 4 lb. as the weight of a magazine of 47 rounds, it will be possible to carry some sixty magazines representing nearly 3,000 rounds. The usual manner of employing such a weapon on a moving target, as presented by an aeroplane in flight, is to fire by "bursts," each burst being sighted afresh and commonly consisting of some six or eight shots, so that the speed of fire never averages as high as that of which the gun is capable; thus the supply of ammunition above given would be sufficient for a continuous and hot engagement of about a quarter of an hour's duration. From the point of view of recoil the machine-gun is quite harmless; the mean recoil of the Lewis gun firing Mark VII. ammunition amounts to slightly less than 2·5 lb. per shot per second, or at 600 per minute the recoil reaction is about 25 lb.

§ 48. *Rapid Fire, Machine-Guns Multiply Mounted.* In view of the advantages of rapid fire, it would seem desirable to increase the speed of fire of the machine-gun to the maximum extent possible. When, on land, the obvious thing to do under similar circumstances would be to bring two guns into action, a similar course is not possible on a flying machine, owing to the weight of the additional gunner. An extra man must either mean the sacrifice of a couple of thousand rounds of ammunition or a couple of hours' petrol supply, neither of which alternatives can be entertained. The conditions indicate the mounting of machine-guns in pairs, or the design of double or triple-barrel guns, the breech actions of which would be independent, but so arranged that they could be fired one, two, or three at a time; by this means a "burst" of twenty-five or thirty bullets could be got off in less than one second. It may be found that a gun designed to take the 0.45 service revolver or automatic-pistol ammunition will be better suited to the conditions than the present weapon, in which the service rifle (Mark VII.) ammunition is employed. Such a gun would be far more handy, owing to the shortness of the cartridge, and would be furnished with a comparatively short barrel; also the magazine could be made of more compact form better to permit of the multiple-barrel design. Beyond the above, the shattering effect of the round-nose pistol bullet is known to be far greater than that of the 0.303 spitzer, so that greater injury will be inflicted on any spars or other structural members that may be hit.

§ 48   AIRCRAFT IN WARFARE.

Incidentally, also, the stopping effect on pilot or gunner will be greater in the event of a shot getting home. In addition to the advantages enumerated, the 0.450 pistol ammunition weighs 21 to the pound, against the service rifle 17, which gives an addition of 25 per cent. to the number of rounds. When drawing on a limited supply of ammunition it is clearly necessary to select whatever is best suited to the work in hand.

PLATE VII.

R.A.F. TYPE R.E.5. An "R.E. Portable" Tent Pole is shown used as Derrick for dismounting Engine

CHAPTER VIII.
(October 23rd, 1914).

RAPIDITY OF FIRE AND ITS MEASURE.
ARMOUR IN ITS RELATION TO ARMAMENT.

§ 49. *Rapidity of Fire and its Measure.* The measure of the rapidity of gun-fire from an aeroplane or dirigible as an index of its fighting value depends upon the nature of the objective or target. It is evident that in some cases the mere number of projectiles per minute is the most important factor, as, for example, in attacking any object in which a hit is a hit whether the projectile be large or small. In other cases, where the mischief done is in any reasonable relation to the weight of the projectile, the *total weight* of projectiles discharged per second (or per minute) affords a better criterion. In view of the comparatively flimsy and fragile nature of aircraft, it is doubtful whether the *energy equivalent* of the discharge will ever be of the importance which it is in the case of the battleship, where the destruction of the enemy depends to a very large extent upon the number of foot-tons with which he is assailed. Thus it is doubtful whether a factor representing the horse-power of the offensive armament would, as applied to the fighting aeroplane, will have any useful significance. Now it is scarcely probable that in the immediate future the fighting-machine can be furnished with complete bullet-proof protection, at least such as can be considered effective at short range. Consequently we may take it that it is quite unimportant whether the bullets used in its destruction be of the usual British 215 grains or the

§ 49 AIRCRAFT IN WARFARE.

162 grains of the Mannlicher, or the 530 grains of the old Enfield. The advantage of size and weight only becomes important when a single hit is sufficient to carry away an important strut or structural member which would have been penetrated without great injury by a bullet of ordinary size. Thus, so long as we are dealing with ordinary rifle, pistol, or machine-gun fire, we are concerned merely with the number of bullets that can be discharged per unit time, and this number—*i.e.*, number per minute or second—fairly and properly expresses the value of the armament. This, of course, does not mean that the weight and muzzle energy of the bullets are of no importance whatever; it is merely an expression of the fact that with such weapons as are commonly available the differences, such as they are, and important though they may be in other applications, are not appreciable in relation to attack by aircraft on aircraft.

§ 50. *Measure of Fire Value in the case of Explosive Projectiles.* When we pass to the consideration of weapons capable of throwing explosive projectiles, it is impossible to maintain, or even suggest, any direct basis of comparison. The effectiveness of shell fire depends entirely upon the conditions being present necessary to the correct timing of the fuse—that is to say, either the range must be known with great accuracy and the time-fuse mechanism correspondingly perfect, or the nature of the target must be such as to permit of the effective employment of an impact fuse of some description. Granted that the necessary conditions exist, the destruction wrought by any given type of explosive projectile may be taken as, in a measure, proportional to its weight. However, there are cases when a 3 lb. high explosive shell would be just as effective as one of 18 lb., as, for example, if it were to strike the motor or fuselage of an aeroplane in flight, and so, in assesssing the value of shell-fire by the aggregate weight of the projectiles thrown, it is evident that we should only be making an approximation to the truth.

If we go further and endeavour to compare the relative value of armament of diverse type for aeroplanes, as, for example, in computing the relative merits of machine-guns and small artillery in any given case, we are inevitably thrown back on examining the service for which the armament is required; it is impossible to institute a direct quantitative comparison which would be generally applicable. If it be conceded that in any particular case a given weight in the form of shell is of greater effect than the same weight in the form of bullets, then we have a *prima facie* case for the use of artillery. If, on the other hand, it is conceded that the bullets would do the greater mischief, then a machine-gun armament is indicated. However, although the weight of ammunition is a matter of first importance, the weight saving and convenience of the machine-gun in itself are sufficient to give it a preference where the other advantages are not overwhelmingly against it.

§ 51. *Weight thrown per minute; Machine-Gun and One-Pounder Compared.* It has in the preceding paragraph been rather assumed that the capacity of the armament, as represented by its weight-rapidity factor of fire, is a constant; this is a matter that depends, firstly, upon the mechanism of the gun. The Lewis gun, which has been taken throughout these articles as representative of the machine-gun in its aeroplane usage, will fire as an ordinary maximum 600 rounds, or 18½ lb. of lead per minute. Unfortunately, there is no standard 1 pounder with which to institute a comparison. The 37-mm. gun is given by different makers as throwing in some cases a projectile 1 lb., and by others the same bore is given as throwing 1½ lb. Also the question arises whether an

§ 51   AIRCRAFT IN WARFARE.

automatic gun of this size is, on account of its heavy mean recoil, an altogether workable proposition. The Vickers automatic 37-mm., for example, is made in two weights; one of these throws a 1 lb. shell at 1,800 foot-seconds at 300 rounds per minute, at which speed of discharge the recoil reaction would be about 300 lb. The weight of this gun is given as 3¾ cwt. This gun is quite unsuited to aeroplane service, both from the point of view of recoil and weight; there is, however, a lighter type by the same firm, of the same calibre, semi-automatic, throwing a 1¼ lb. projectile with a velocity of 1,200 ft. per second, the weight of the gun being given as 110 lb. Presumably the maximum rate of fire of this gun would be about thirty rounds per minute, or the weight of metal thrown per minute, 45 lb. This is about 2½ times the weight per minute given above for the machine-gun.

§ 52. *Weight per minute as limited by Recoil.* Quite apart from mechanical details, however, a real limiting factor exists in the *recoil reaction* to the momentum per second permissible, and this limit may be taken as applying whatever the type of gun may be; consequently, since the muzzle velocity of one type and another is not widely different, the weight discharged per second or per minute will have an approximate maximum for any particular aeroplane no matter what the type of gun may be. This is the reason why it is possible and, in the author's opinion, advantageous to employ duplication, or even fit three or four barrels in the case of the machine-gun; whereas an automatic 1-pounder under like conditions could not reasonably be allowed to fire at over 60 or 80 rounds per minute.

§ 53. *Present Advantage of Machine Guns. Future Possibilities discussed.* At present there are very few cases in which the automatic or semi-automatic 1-pounder could compete with the machine-gun as an aeroplane arm.

ARMOUR IN RELATION TO ARMAMENT.   § 53

If a percussion or impact-fuse were available sufficiently sensitive to explode with certainty on encountering balloon-cloth, the 1-pounder would be an excellent weapon for the destruction of the airship or dirigible. Every part of a shell exploding within the envelope is effective, and the fragments of a shell leave wounds in the envelope and give rise to loss of gas of a more serious character than that due to the rifle or machine-gun bullet. Beyond this the danger to the crew (and structure in the case of a Zeppelin) is considerably greater under these conditions than under equivalent machine-gun fire. It may be some time, however, before the impact-fuse reaches the required degree of perfection.

In the author's opinion there is room for a well-designed light-weight automatic to fire 14-oz. shell at a moderate velocity, say 1,200 ft. per second, with a maximum rate of 100 rounds per minute, the weight of the gun to be kept, if possible, under 100 lb; the length should be kept as short as the requirements of the internal ballistics permit. The value of such a weapon, however, would depend almost entirely upon the development of suitable ammunition, and in particular, as already pointed out, the perfection of the impact-fuse to a point not yet within sight.

§ 54. *Armour in its relation to Armament.* We have already given considerable attention to the question of armour in connection with the primary function of the aeronautical Arm—the attack on and co-operation with the other Arms of the Service. It is now time to extend our study to the secondary function of the Arm, and discuss the question in relation to problems of aerial attack and defence. The first instalment of the conditions which need to be fulfilled by the aeroplane constructor arises directly from the consideration of the primary function; thus, it is already given us that the armament

§ 54   AIRCRAFT IN WARFARE.

to be of maximum service must be capable of action to the full in a downward direction with the greatest angle of fire (both forward and aft, and laterally), that the limitations imposed by structural considerations permit. Similarly, we know that the initial need for armour is mainly to resist attack from below. These facts remain, and cannot be altered by the additional duties imposed when aeroplane attacks aeroplane. We may, and in fact shall, have to provide for a far wider range of fire; we shall need to make provision for training our gun or guns upward as well as downward; likewise we may find it expedient to provide protection against fire from above as well as beneath. But any extended scheme of armament or protection so developed takes essentially as its starting point the more elementary condition.

§ 55. *Importance of Upper "Gage" or Berth.* The first result of importance arising from the above facts is, in any aeronautical engagement, the *importance of the upper berth*. The machine which is able to attack from above is acting under the conditions for which its armour and armament were initially provided. Beyond this, the taking of the upper position at the start, or perhaps, we may say, before the start, gives the power to outmanoeuvre an enemy, in spite even of inferior speed capacity in the ordinary acceptation of the term. The initial difference in altitude represents a store of potential energy which may be drawn upon when the opportunity occurs; this is, in fact, the principle utilised by the hawk, the kite, and other birds of prey. The objective of securing the upper berth, or position, or "gage," if we adopt the old-time word used by naval writers, will probably prove to be, and will remain, the key or pivot on which every scheme of aeronautical tactics will, in some way or another, be found to hang.

THE UPPER "GAGE": ATTACK FROM ABOVE. § 56

§ 56. *On Protection against Attack from Above.* The question of employing armour as a protection against attack from above, or against dropping fire, is one which requires consideration on an entirely different basis from that of attack from below. In the latter case, the employment of protection in some degree may be looked upon as essential. The steel employed may be thin and only sufficient to be effective above some prearranged altitude, but, nevertheless, it will be essential. Protection from attack by other aeroplanes, or, more broadly, aircraft, is another question; we may express the utility of armour under these conditions definitely in terms of gun-power.

To make this clear let us consider two machines in combat—an aeroplane duel, in fact—and we will take it that at their average distance apart or range the mean number of shots fired by either to score a decisive hit is found to be 600. Now if either aeronaut by the employment of armour or gun-shields, or equivalent device, can reduce the effective target offered by his machine to one-half that previously presented, it will on an average take 1,200 shots to knock him out in lieu of 600 without protection. But in order to provide for the weight of his armour he must cut down his armament; he must sacrifice either his gun weight, and with it his speed of fire, or he must carry a lesser total weight of ammunition, and risk finding himself without means of attack, this being virtually synonymous to being without means of defence. If the only alternative were the cutting down of the speed of fire—tersely, if he were to substitute, say, 30 lb. of armour for 30 lb. of gun—and if this represent half his total gun capacity, and involve a reduction in his speed of fire by nearly one-half, then the change might be considered as *nearly* justified, since he would receive two shots for every one he could discharge, but would at the same time be proportionately less vulnerable.

§ 56   AIRCRAFT IN WARFARE.

Obviously, *rate of fire* should be one of the last things to be sacrificed; but the alternative—a reduction in the load of ammunition—involves a curtailment of the period of activity, and, as a corollary, an increase in the number of machines required for a given combatant duty. Once admit the necessity for such additional machines, and we must estimate the sacrifice, or price paid for the armour, in terms of the loss of fighting strength due to the absence of a section of the air-fleet occupied in replenishing. This is evidently a serious matter under the best conditions—*i.e.*, when fighting in the immediate vicinity of the base; if, however, an air-fleet be engaged far afield it becomes still more serious, and the sacrifice of rapidity of fire, rather than reserve of ammunition, might well prove to be the lesser of evils.

The foregoing illustration shows that, tangibly or intangibly, the matter is one of figures, or, at the worst, a balance of advantages not capable of ready numerical expression. It may thus not always be possible to lay it down definitely whether in theory given conditions mean the abandonment of armour or otherwise; but nevertheless the fact is determined by the sum of the conditions, and where theory is dumb the decision will require to be taken on actual experience, as in analogous problems in naval construction.

§ 57. *Protection by Armour and Shield Contrasted.* It is, perhaps, opportune to draw attention here to the difference between *shield* and *armour* as a means of protection. The shield is essentially mobile, it is moved round and about to give the best protection possible, according to the direction of attack. A shield commonly forms part of a gun-mounting, but this is by way of being an accidental circumstance; the gun has to be trained on the enemy, and so the shield is made part and parcel of the gun, thus automatically taking the best position

PROTECTION BY ARMOUR AND SHIELD. § 57

for the gunner's protection. In the aeroplane, however, the pilot is of almost more importance than the gunner; hence this traditional method of handling the shield may not be the best possible arrangement; perhaps it will be found advantageous to provide the pilot with a shield separately mounted or otherwise adjustable. There is rarely any intention in the case of a shield to give full and complete protection as is done with armour. It is an error to suppose that partial protection is of no value; every square inch covered diminishes proportionally the chances of a fatal hit, and so increases the fighting value of the machine, just as would a commensurate increase in rapidity of gun-fire; on the other hand, as already insisted, either armour or shield which is insufficient in thickness is worse than useless.

It is probable that in cases in which it may not pay to fit armour, it will still be found profitable, owing to the considerations already discussed, to provide shields to give partial protection both to gunner and pilot.

CHAPTER IX.
(October 30th, 1914).

GUN-FIRE BALLISTICS. THE ENERGY ACCOUNT.
EXPANDING AND EXPLOSIVE BULLETS.

§ 58. *Gun-Fire. The Energy Account.* The kinetic energy of a projectile commonly represents from 10 to 30 per cent. of the total energy of the explosive or powder charge by which it is projected; the lower figure corresponds to the performance of a small-bore low-velocity rifle such as a rook rifle, the latter being that approached under the most favourable conditions by the military or big-game rifle. The British Service rifle with Mark VI. ammunition thus has an efficiency of approximately 28 per cent.; in the ordinary sportsman's "12-bore" the figure is about 11 per cent.

The total energy released on combustion by black powder is the equivalent in round numbers of 500 foot-tons per pound. The corresponding figure in the case of cordite is half as much again, approximately 750 foot-tons per pound; in general it may be taken that most of the explosives in common use have an energy content between 500 and 1,000 foot-tons per pound. In the case of the Service rifle with Mark VI. ammunition the weight of the powder (cordite) is 30 grains (0.0043 lb.), and the bullet 215 grains (0.0307 lb.), the velocity being 2,050 ft. per second. Thus the total energy of the charge is $0.0043 \times 750 = 3.2$ foot-tons, and the muzzle (kinetic) energy is 2,000 foot-pounds $= 0.895$ foot-ton; the efficiency, therefore, is $0.895/3.2 = 0.28$, as already given. It is worthy of remark, *en passant*, that there is

GUNFIRE: ENERGY OF PROJECTILE. § 58

very close accord between the figures applying to the gun and those which obtain in the gas-engine. In all such matters as efficiency, heat lost to barrel (cylinder walls), and heat remaining in gases; the agreement is far closer than one would have ventured to expect in view of the great disparity of the conditions.

§ 59. *Energy Available and Otherwise.* It has already been pointed out that under the conditions of attack on aircraft there is very little possibility of utilising the whole of the energy of the bullet on impact. Unless the motor mechanism, or the pilot or gunner, be hit, the character of the structure employed in aircraft is such that the bullet or projectile will pass through with a comparatively insignificant loss of energy and will do little or no damage. With the ordinary military bullet, and more particularly with the spitzer model, nothing less than encounter with a heavy metal part will cause it to break up. Any non-metallic structural material, such as timber, is bored cleanly through, and if initially designed with a reasonable margin of safety, the resulting injury to it is negligible. The position is similar to that which existed, before the adoption of explosive shell, in the attack on the wooden ship by the artillery or cannon of a century ago. At close quarters the cannon ball would go clean through, often with comparatively little injury. It is said that Napoleon, observing this to be the case, himself expressed the opinion that explosive shell (a then well-known expedient in siege operations) could be adopted generally in naval warfare with advantage. The situation is considerably more acute in the case of the attack on aircraft by rifle-fire, and so we are led to consider the possibilities of the explosive or expanding bullet, ignoring, for the purpose of discussion, the existence of the Declaration of St. Petersburg.

§ 60 AIRCRAFT IN WARFARE.

§ 60. *The Explosive Bullet.* The simplest form of explosive bullet, and one of the most effective, is that devised by Mr. Metford about the middle of the last century; this, as applied to an Enfield bullet of the period 1860, is illustrated in Fig. 11. An explosive charge is inserted in the fore part of the bullet, and consists of equal parts of sulphur and chlorate of potash,* this mixture acting both as detonator and "burster." The hollow-ended form, or "drilled-up" end, has the incidental advantage that it alone will determine the

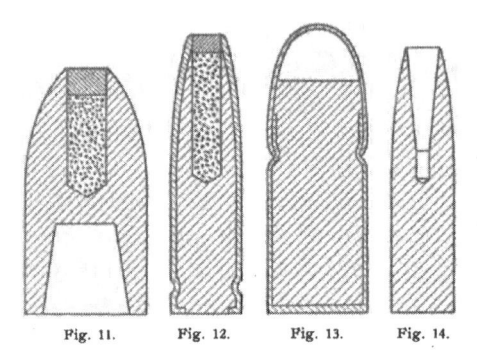

Fig. 11.   Fig. 12.   Fig. 13.   Fig. 14.

expansion of the bullet on impact, quite apart from the action of the explosive charge. If the Metford system were applied to the modern bullet, the section would be somewhat as shown in Fig. 12, the basis of which is the Service 0.303 Mark VI. Another good form to take as the basis of an explosive bullet is the capped bullet, Fig. 13, as used in sporting rifles, the space inside the cap being conveniently filled with mixture to Metford's specification.

It is difficult, however the cavity be arranged, to devote more than about one-eighth or one-seventh of

* This mixture being liable to detonate by friction, the ingredients require to be separately ground and mixed with due care.

THE EXPLOSIVE BULLET. § 60

the volume of the bullet to receive the charge, and consequently, in view of the relatively low density of the explosive (about 1.6 in the case in point), the weight of the burster cannot be more than some 2 or 3 per cent. of the total. Taking the figure for cordite as representing the energy of the burster explosive, this means, in the case of the Service rifle, about 5 or 8 grains, or 1,300 ft.-lb. energy. But the efficiency of the burster is not likely to be higher than that which we associate with the main charge—it is at some advantage, inasmuch as there is no confined barrel to the walls of which heat is lost, but it is at a serious disadvantage, in that the explosion is not with any certainty confined to its work. It is doubtful whether of the 1,300 ft.-lb. total more than 300 ft.-lb. on an average will be usefully expended.

We are thus led to appreciate the attributes of the explosive bullet, and more generally the explosive shell, in true perspective. The explosive only adds to an initial energy content of 2,000 ft.-lb. as due to velocity, a matter of about 300 ft.-lb. in available explosive energy, a quantity representing an addition of only 15 per cent. It is at once evident that the value of the explosive charge is less due to its direct action than to the fact that by its spreading or scattering effect on the projectile the kinetic energy is used to better advantage. In other words, the explosion is effective as a means of initiating or causing the expansion of the bullet rather than as acting directly by its own destructive power. In the case of large shells the proportion of burster charge to total weight can be increased, and so the direct effect is relatively more important; for armour-piercing projectiles, however, the proportion is no higher than in the example taken—*i.e.*, about 3 per cent. It might be imagined that the employment of some higher explosive would give a capacity of greater direct bursting energy, but the high

§ 60   AIRCRAFT IN WARFARE.

explosive is not so called by reason of any greater total energy content, but rather on the effects of its rapidity of action ; in brief, its power of detonation.

It is evident that, for the purpose under contemplation, the destruction of the less substantial structural parts of aeroplanes, etc., if we are able to secure the proper and immediate expansion of the bullet on impact without the use of an explosive charge, every useful purpose will be served. The bullet energy, even reduced to about one-quarter of its initial value by 1,000 yards flight, is more than sufficient, if definitely expended in the impact, to destroy any strut or spar or other light constructional part, without any aid from an explosive charge. The question is, whether the expansion of the bullet can be induced to take place with sufficient rapidity by any less drastic device.

§ 61. *The Expanding Bullet.* Any bullet is considered an expanding bullet if it be so made as to spread or mushroom on impact with its objective. But it is more usual to restrict the term to bullets having some special provision artificially to assist or facilitate their expansion, and, generally speaking, the objective is assumed to be game or other living quarry of some description. Evidently, if the target be hard enough, every bullet will expand to some degree. The means usually adopted in the case of the solid-lead bullet is to drill or form a hollow in the nose, as familiar to all who have used the sporting rifle. Another well-known method is to split the nose for a short distance by two cuts at right angles. In the case of the nickel-covered bullet the drilled nose again is sometimes adopted, or the nickel sheath at the nose, or point, of the bullet, is removed, the lead core being laid bare. All these devices have been practised in connection with sporting ammunition for many years. The art of designing an expanding

THE EXPANDING BULLET. § 61

bullet is so to proportion things that under the average conditions the degree of expansion is that found to be most desirable ; thus the depth of the hole, or the extent of the slits, or the amount of the sheath cut away may be varied to whatever extent desired. The object to be attained is that the bullet shall expend its whole energy in inflicting the maximum possible injury, but at the same time it must not go to pieces or spread to such an extent that its penetration is lacking. In stopping big game it is necessary, not only that the energy should be wholly utilised, but also that it should be expended, as far as possible, in injury to the deep-seated vital organs. More recently Messrs. Westley Richards have brought out a modified form of expanding bullet in which the sheath is kept intact, but is not wholly filled by the lead core, there being an air-space in the fore end; this type (already illustrated in Fig. 13), expands to a moderate degree only, and retains a considerable power of penetration.

§ 62. *Expansion due to Centrifugal Force.* One of the main factors contributing to the spreading or expansion of a bullet is the centrifugal force of the bullet itself; all that is required of the impact is so to break down the structure of the bullet as *to permit* it to expand. The direction of motion of the peripheral portions of the bullet make at all points an angle with the axis of flight at least equal to the angle of the rifling, which is commonly about 1 in 10 to 1 in 12. This is the state of things when the bullet is discharged, but the actual angle rapidly becomes greater owing to the reduction of velocity, the speed of rotation being comparatively little affected. Thus at 1,000 yards range the velocity is reduced by half, and the relative direction of the skin of the bullet becomes about 1 in 6 to the line of flight. If then by a sudden impact or other means the bullet be

§ 62   AIRCRAFT IN WARFARE.

broken into a number of small fragments at any point in its path, these fragments immediately spread out after the manner of shrapnel, covering a cone whose base is approximately one-third of its height; moreover, the distribution of the fragments in space—that is, within the conical surface—will be almost uniform. Such a distribution is almost ideal from the point of view of the work in hand. A desirable solution to the problem would appear to lie in the direction of a bullet composed of pellets or shot embedded in a matrix of only just sufficient strength to hold together, so that on comparatively light impact the component pellets will be released, and each will follow its individual direction of motion.

In every case the degree of expansibility requires, finally, to be determined by experiment, though with sufficient previous experience, and a proper comprehension of the conditions, it is usually possible to hit off the right thing without much difficulty. For the destruction of wooden struts, spars, etc., it is clearly necessary to obtain the most rapid expansion possible (corresponding to instant disintegration), since the bullet has to do its work in a distance rarely exceeding some 3 in. or 4 in. Owing to the fact that the "tissue" penetrated is of very low density—about 30 lb. or 40 lb. per cubic ft.—it is probable that good results would be obtained by drilling the nose with a conical aperture of large diameter, at the entrance about half the diameter of the bullet, after the manner illustrated in Fig. 14. The author is at the present time making a series of experiments with expansive bullets on a target made up of wooden scantlings of cross-section comparable to aeroplane struts or wing members. We may form some estimate of the latent destructive power of the military Service bullet from the fact that it will penetrate some 4 ft. of deal or pine, representing 3½ cubic inches of wood *displaced*. Taking this as a criterion, it is clear that if we can obtain the necessary rapidity of expansion, there is ample energy in a single hit to sever any ordinary wing or similar structural member.

§ 63. *The Light Weight Shell.* Apart from the question of the explosive or expansible bullet, we have already seen that the 14 oz. limit of projectile weight is an irksome restriction when we are dealing with aeroplane armament. Not only is the gun required weighty and cumbersome, but the weight of the ammunition is, save for machines of exceptional size, almost prohibitive. If we are able to adopt a weight of 6 oz. or 8 oz. in place of 14 oz., it will be possible to use a gun direct-mounted without the elaboration of recoil mechanism, and weighing from 40 lb. to 45 lb. In addition to this, the cartridges would weigh less than 1 lb. apiece, and provision could be made for some 300 rounds in a machine of present-day dimensions. For attack on other aeroplanes, such a shell would be almost as effective as one of twice the weight, and, owing to the recoil limit, the rate of fire can be doubled if the lighter shell be adopted.

It is convenient to make a distinction between the *explosive bullet* and the *shell*, even if the definition be considered somewhat artificial. The former is defined as containing a single charge, impact fuse and "burster" in one ; the latter (the shell) contains, as well as the burster charge, an independent cap or detonator, and a fuse or mechanism, time or impact, for determining the instant of explosion. Many writers refer to the explosive bullet equally as a shell.

It is unnecessary to discuss the probability or possibility of the abandonment of the restriction imposed by the Declaration of St. Petersburg. We know that the clause in question was framed from humanitarian

§ 63 AIRCRAFT IN WARFARE.

motives, and it is fairly evident that any expanding bullet which, from its behaviour, is tantamount to an explosive bullet, may be looked upon as infringing the terms of the Declaration, even though it contain no actual explosive; the terms of the Hague Declaration (Article 60) are virtually an admission of this. It is equally clear that neither at St. Petersburg, in 1868, nor at the Hague, in 1899, did the matter arise that now confronts us; and so it is actually a question to what extent either document will be considered binding under the conditions which have arisen. In any case it behoves us to ascertain everything there is to know on the subject, and to be prepared for all eventualities.

CHAPTER X.
(November 6th, 1914).

MISCELLANEOUS WEAPONS AND MEANS OF OFFENCE.
SUPREMACY OF THE GUN.

§ 64. *Other Weapons of Offence.* For the fighting aeroplane there is no doubt that the gun will prove to be the most useful all-round weapon; however, several other means of offence have been suggested and to some extent have proved themselves of value. Bombs and hand-grenades, both explosive and incendiary, have been found to be of considerable service under appropriate conditions. Other means of attack have been proposed, such as rockets, air-borne torpedoes, etc.; so far, neither of these latter appears to have been successfully utilised.

The difference between a bomb and a hand-grenade is mainly a matter of size and weight, and a corresponding difference in the arrangements made for its release. Ordinarily, a hand-grenade is a small bomb of some 5 lb. or 6 lb. weight or less, containing a high explosive or inflammable charge, and is, as its name implies, thrown by hand. Requiring no particular provision for its storage or discharge, it is a weapon particularly suited to employment by scouting and other machines not primarily intended for fighting. The judicious employment of a few hand-grenades for the scattering of cavalry or the stampeding of led horses, or against troops on the march or massed in reserve, may by its effect amply justify the use of such a device. The bomb is commonly of considerably larger dimensions than the hand-grenade, and is stored or mounted in a magazine of some kind

§ 64   AIRCRAFT IN WARFARE.

beneath the fuselage of the machine, with some mechanical device for its release, arranged either to let go a single bomb or to empty the magazine as required. It may be said that whereas the hand-grenade, in common with the machine-gun, is only suitable for injuring *personnel*, the legitimate objective of the bomb is *matériel*. Thus the dépôts, magazines, arsenals, oil stores, etc., of the enemy cannot be effectively destroyed by gun-fire, at least from present-day aircraft; but if attacked by a few squadrons of aeroplanes, each dropping some eight or ten 30-lb. or 40-lb. bombs, irreparable mischief might be effected in a very short space of time.

We may take it that in the future any such points will be duly protected by the fighting aeroplanes of the enemy. Consequently the bomb-dropping machine will need to be also a fighting machine itself, with a capacity for rapid fire sufficient to enable it to hold its own with the enemy. Or it will need to act in conjunction with a supporting fleet of fighting machines of sufficient strength to overpower, or at least hold, the enemy during the operation.

It is thus clear that the bomb differs from the hand grenade in not being a weapon suitable for casual employment by the reconnaissance machine. Further than this, it is a weapon which will in future warfare probably be found to possess comparatively little value, except when used in considerable numbers by machines acting in squadrons, or fleets several squadrons strong. The use of the incendiary bomb, or petrol bomb, as it is sometimes termed, is indicated where the objective is of a sufficiently inflammable character. But it is probable that in all cases in which an attack is made upon buildings of permanent character, such as in the destruction of an arms or ammunition factory, or of a dockyard, the petrol bomb will be used to complete the

HAND GRENADES AND BOMBS. § 64

job by firing the wreckage remaining after high explosives have done their work.

§ 65. *The Bomb: Difficulties in Connection with Aiming.* The accurate directing or aiming of bombs or hand-grenades, or of any gravitationally-propelled missile, is one of great difficulty, and many suggestions for the improvement of the degree of precision attainable have been made. The problem, in a sense, is the inverse of that of firing at an aeroplane at high altitude. The period during which the projectile is at the top of its trajectory (the beginning of its fall in the case of the bomb), and in which its velocity is low, introduces considerable uncertainty as to direction; it has been proposed to minimise this difficulty by giving the bomb an initial velocity or "send off," by some form of spring or pneumatic gun. The factor affecting the aim definitely known to the pilot is the velocity of flight (relatively to the air); the factors less exactly known are the height, the direction and velocity of the wind, or, as it must be reckoned by the aeronaut, the *earth drift*, and the direction of the vertical. Previous observation may have given the approximate wind allowance, and the barometric reading (the aneroid) will give the altitude, which, in conjunction with a contour map, will give the pilot the figure for his height. The determination of the vertical, or "plumb," is far less simple or certain than may at first sight appear, since any pendulum device is affected by acceleration just as much as by gravity, and the reading of a damped pendulum or a spirit-level gives the *apparent* plumb, which may be literally *anywhere*.

In the case of a machine "looping the loop," for example, the apparent plumb is, in fact, at one instant diametrically opposite to the true plumb, and during the whole evolution it "boxes the compass" in a vertical plane. The lateral deviations of the apparent from the true plumb, are no less serious, and, whenever a machine is turning and correctly banked, the spirit-level records the machine as being on an even keel. In other words, an error in the reading under these conditions is equal to the angle of banking, and is quite commonly as much as 30 deg. or 40 deg. It is precisely on this point—the confusion of the true with the apparent plumb—that many of the suggestions offered for the direction of bomb-dropping are found to fail; and it is quite useless for those having no knowledge of the principles involved to attempt to deal with the problem. No better way of obtaining a clear conception of the difficulty exists than a study of the pendulum accelerometer.*

In the case of a modern aeroplane which virtually "flies itself" it is possible to determine the true plumb with considerable exactitude under calm atmospheric conditions. Such a machine will, just like a gliding model, settle down to a definite flight velocity, known as its natural velocity, and to a known gliding angle, and will maintain a tolerably straight path; under these circumstances the apparent plumb *is* the true plumb. When, however, atmospheric disturbances are present, the difficulty once more makes it appearance.

In view of the above, it is doubtful whether bomb-dropping from aeroplanes will ever be found to compete with gun-fire on the score of accuracy, and it may be anticipated that the utility of this mode of offence will be confined mainly to attack on positions or objects that present a mark either of sufficient area or size to be easily hit, or of sufficient importance to justify a disproportionate expenditure of missiles.

* *Philosophical Magazine*, August, 1905; also Proceedings of the Institution of Automobile Engineers, vol. iv., page 124.

THE STEEL DART. § 66

§ 66. *The Steel Dart.* A form of gravitational projectile or missile introduced during the present war is the steel dart; this commonly consists of a piece of steel wire or rod some 5 in. or 6 in. long by $\frac{1}{8}$ in. in diameter, pointed at the one end and "feathered" at the other. In size and shape the missile resembles and ordinary well-sharpened graphite pencil, the feathering being done in some cases by the milling away of the tail portion to a cruciform section; alternatively the rear two-thirds of the missile may be made of thin-gauge tube. The weight is about 1 oz. This "pencil dart" is used against the *personnel* of the enemy—*i.e.*, encampments, men or cavalry on the march, etc.; the rate of fall, if dropped from a few thousand feet altitude, would be little short of the limiting velocity, say some 400 ft. or 500 ft. per second. The penetration at this velocity should be equal to several inches of spruce planking. Steel darts are either allowed to fall out of a hopper or may be simply thrown out or "sown" by hand. They appear to be quite effective when they find their mark, but their discharge and direction are subject to the same limitations as to accuracy which apply to the throwing of the hand-grenade or bomb, with much greater uncertainty as due to air resistance. Beyond this the steel dart, to be effective, *must* be dropped from a height—a very considerable height—and so it is not possible to make a sudden descent for the purpose of bringing off an attack, as is the case when the bomb is the weapon chosen. For these reasons the author does not believe that the dart will have a very great vogue. Once the aeroplane has been satisfactorily adapted to the carrying of a machine-gun, it is quite clear that the steel dart, weighing, as it does, as much as the ordinary Service cartridge, must be regarded as a weapon of doubtful utility.

§ 67   AIRCRAFT IN WARFARE.

§ 67. *The Rocket and the Air-Borne Torpedo.* A suggestion which has been made over and over again is that of the employment of the rocket in some shape or form; the objective is usually presumed to be a dirigible or airship, and the rocket is to be fired from a rocket-tube or gun of some kind from an attacking aeroplane. There are two replies to this suggestion: firstly, no weapon can be contemplated as forming part of an aeroplane armament which is *confined in its purpose* to the attacking of the airship. The airship is already being regarded as a prospective *bonne bouche* for the aeroplane squadron fortunate enough to encounter it in the open, and, as the recent exploit at Düsseldorf has shown, it is not in a much happier condition when at home. It is already recognised that the airship may not expose itself to the attentions of hostile aeroplanes, and when the latter are able to attack by one-pounder shell fire, in addition to bombs (explosive and incendiary), the airship, already little more than a name in active hostilities, will cease to have any, even verbal, interest. Apart from the above, the supposed effectiveness of the rocket, or of other spit-fire projectile, is based to a great extent upon a misconception. The modern airship is not so easily set on fire as is commonly supposed; in the rigid type, as exemplified in the Zeppelin, it is reported that the space between the gas-bags and the outer envelope is charged with a non-flammable gas, and it may be penetrated by any ordinary rocket through and through without the smallest chance of ignition.*

The aerial torpedo (proposed by the author in 1897) at first sight appears promising. Such a torpedo would consist of a gliding model of high velocity adapted to be

---

* This feature was actually proposed some years ago to the authorities in this country, and was understood to be a matter of secrecy. However, according to *Navy and Army Illustrated* (September 12, 1914), it now appears to be an established feature of some of the later German Zeppelins.

launched from a gun or pneumatic projector of some kind, and carrying a charge of explosive and an impact fuse actuated by the striking of the aerofoil member on some part of the enemy's craft. Again, we are confronted with the fact that any such weapon would be of little service apart from attack on an airship, and so may be looked upon as useless lumber.

§ 68. *The Supremacy of the Gun.* The real fact at the bottom of the whole question is the vital importance of high velocity in any projectile directed against a rapidly moving target, and its doubly vital importance when the craft from which it is projected is also in rapid motion. This is universally recognised wherever the gun is to be found, and it is nowhere more important than in the attack on aircraft by aircraft, and in particular aeroplane on aeroplane. Any lapse of time whilst the projectile is in its flight introduces a corresponding uncertainty owing to the relative difference of motion between gun and mark. Thus a projectile travelling at 200 ft. or 300 ft. per second, such as a rocket or aerial torpedo, would require to be directed at a point so far removed from the aircraft it is intended to hit, that, in the case of an aeroplane, the chances of success would be remote in the extreme.

In brief, nothing but gun-fire gives the necessary rapidity to ensure a reasonable degree of accuracy and useful percentage of hits, and it is probable that for some time to come the demand will be for higher and higher velocity in order that the effective range may be increased. This, however, is looking into the future; at present, the problem of mounting a gun in a satisfactory manner, and getting the highest possible rate of discharge—*i.e.*, rounds per minute—are the more immediate concern of the aeroplane constructor. The relation of the ordinary flight velocity to the mean

§ 68   AIRCRAFT IN WARFARE.

velocity of the projectile is round about 12 to 1, and this gives the angle of lead necessary to aim in front of the objective from a fixed mounting. When firing from another aeroplane moving in the opposite direction, the angle of lead will be six to one more or less, a considerably greater allowance than is known in any other branch of gunnery. With the highest muzzle velocity and slow-moving aircraft the angle of lead under these conditions is about 1 in 15. The angle of lead given by a pigeon-shot when the bird is flying fast across the line-of-sight is about 1 in 20, and even here the demand, under the stress of competition, is for higher and higher velocity. This may be taken as a sure indication of what may be expected in the eventual future of aeronautical gunnery.

CHAPTER XI.
(November 13th, 1914).

AIRCRAFT IN THE SERVICE OF THE NAVY.

§ 69. *Naval Aircraft. Special Conditions.* The position of aircraft in connection with naval warfare requires to be studied almost as an independent problem, since many of the circumstances and conditions are utterly different from those which obtain on land. Apart from differences in the constructional features which, particularly in the case of the aeroplane, are considerable, the questions which arise in the matter of attack and defence are so entirely modified, at least as affecting the primary function of the arm, as to influence fundamentally the question of armament. Thus gun-fire, except as against hostile aircraft, ceases to have any appreciable value; no gun capable of being mounted in any aeroplane or dirigible at present built, or contemplated, would be of the slightest service directed against even the smallest unit of the enemy's navy. Again, when we consider the duties of reconnaisance, we are faced with totally altered conditions. In the case of the aeroplane, so long as we are confined to bases situated on or near the coast, the area which can be reconnoitred is limited to a distance of some 300 or 400 miles (possibly 500 miles) from the coast-line, this being at present an altogether outside estimate. Since we commonly have to regard our frontier as defined by the limit of the enemy's territorial waters, it is clear that any such restriction is

§ 69   AIRCRAFT IN WARFARE.

to be considered inadmissible. In the case of the large airship, especially the rigid type, the range or radius of action is usually taken to be considerably greater, possibly some 1,000 miles as an extreme. If we admit this (crediting the dirigible with more reliability than it has yet exhibited), we are still faced with the fact that such a machine cannot operate with safety in the presence of, or within the zone patrolled by, the enemy's aeroplanes.

§ 70. *Mother-ship or Floating Base.* So far as the scouting aeroplane is concerned, the obvious solution to the difficulty is the provision of a floating aeroplane base, capable of accompanying, or acting in co-operation with, the fleet on the high seas, or of acting independently if required. Various schemes in this direction have been proposed; the future appears to lie between a "mother-ship" adapted to take on board the necessary complement of aeroplanes (or "seaplanes" as they are frequently termed when fitted with floats), and to fulfil the functions of storage, transport, and supply; and a more thorough-going scheme in which the floating base takes the form of a specialised vessel with a clear deck of sufficient area to permit of machines being launched or alighting without entering the water at all. In the former scheme the normal condition is that the machines are lowered into the water from which they are required to rise, and on which, in due course, they alight; in the latter the machines are not presumed to enter the water at all, any immersion is by way of being an accident, for which eventuality, however, the machines would be adapted by being furnished with floats in addition to the ordinary landing gear. To be effective a quite special design of vessel would be necessary, with a completely clear and flush upper deck. In order to obtain the requisite area it would probably be necessary to design something comparable in dimensions to one of the largest of our existing

ARMAMENT OF THE NAVAL AEROPLANE. § 70

battle-cruisers, and in particular the maximum beam possible should be provided. A closer study of this problem will be given in a later chapter.

§ 71. *The Armament of the Naval Aeroplane. The Employment of Bombs.* Dealing for the time being entirely with the primary function of the Aeronautical Arm in the service of the Navy, we have already pointed out that the gun, whether the machine-gun or the one-pounder, is of no value whatever. Hence, if the aeroplane or the airship is to possess any power of offence at all against the ships of the enemy, it must be sought elsewhere. A great deal has been said on the subject of bomb-dropping as a means of attack on armoured ships, but it is not as well recognised as it should be how comparatively impotent a bomb, even charged with high explosive, may be when used without "tamping" against armour-plate. It is quite true that a certain amount of mischief would be wrought by a bomb of large size if successfully dropped on to the deck of a battleship or cruiser, and the effect would certainly be more disagreeable still if the recipient were a destroyer or some still smaller craft. The effect, however, would in no degree be comparable to that of a torpedo, where the inertia of the surrounding water plays an important *rôle*. It would, in any case, take a vast number of hits to put a first-class battleship or cruiser out of action. Further, the difficulties of aim, as pointed out in the preceding chapter, are considerable, and with the counter-aircraft armament with which warships are now being fitted, it will not, generally speaking, be possible for an aeroplane to descend to low altitude with impunity. The dropping of bombs from an airship is a matter of somewhat less difficulty; moreover, the bombs employed may themselves be of really formidable dimensions; but here the author is of opinion that an airship will not in the future be able

§ 71   AIRCRAFT IN WARFARE.

to approach a warship of any kind by daylight without certain destruction, and it may be little or no better off by night.

§ 72. *Torpedo Attack by Air.* Some experiments reported as having been made in Germany appear to indicate a direction in which aircraft may become an actual source of danger to even the most formidable battleship or cruiser. It is said that a Zeppelin has recently been fitted with means of discharging a Whitehead torpedo with complete success. We may presume that the airship is brought down close to the sea-level, and then fires the torpedo, just as is done from the deck-tube of a torpedo-boat. In view of the great range of the modern torpedo—at the present day over 2 miles—this form of attack cannot be ignored. It is evident that what is possible to the airship in this direction is also possible to the aeroplane, provided that the latter be built of sufficient carrying capacity; and whereas the airship would find it difficult to approach a battleship or cruiser within 2 miles without detection and destruction, the aeroplane would rarely find this either difficult or dangerous; the matter is mainly one of choosing the proper time and direction of attack. In the haze of the early morning, or in the dusk after sunset, an aeroplane at the distance in question is quite invisible; or again, it is frequently possible for an aeroplane to approach in broad daylight against a landscape background without being observed, especially if assisted by suitable protective colouring; much depends also upon the direction of the sun's rays. Night attack would also in many instances be possible, although the absence of light may be a greater hindrance than help to the aeronaut; added to this there is the not inconsiderable risk of being located by searchlight. The aeroplane for the duty in question will need to be somewhat larger and of greater carrying capacity than the present standard; the modern 21-in. torpedo, for example, weighs approximately 1 ton, and would require a machine of about 4 tons gross lifting power. The older model, the 18-in. weapon, weighs about 12 cwt., and would require a machine with a gross lifting-power of 2½ tons, the latter being not very much in excess of the largest machines already in service.

§ 73. *Aeroplane as affected by Discharge of Torpedo.* It might be thought, considering the matter superficially, that the dropping of one-quarter of the gross weight of a machine whilst in flight would be a dangerous and risky business. But closer investigation shows that this is not the case; the resulting disturbance is one which can be quite easily rectified by the pilot. In the case of the modern machine, whose flight path is stable (the *dynamically-stable* machine), and which is said to be—and undoubtedly is—capable of flying itself, the disturbance calculated as due to the release of the torpedo is well within the permissible limit. The only condition to be observed is that the centre of gravity of the machine shall not be thrown forward or backward by the discharge; in other words, the centre of gravity of the torpedo, as carried, must be approximately in the same vertical line as that of the machine. If this condition is complied with, the resulting disturbance, assuming the torpedo as constituting one-quarter of the gross weight, is shown by the diagram Fig. 15. The torpedo being dropped at point p_1, the path of flight $p_1 p_2$ becomes undulatory, the undulations dying out, as indicated in the figure, at a rate depending upon the degree of dynamic stability provided. The extent of the initial undulation is correctly represented to scale in the figure, and is the same as would be produced in a 70-mile-an-hour machine by an adverse wind gust of 10 miles per hour, a thing of everyday

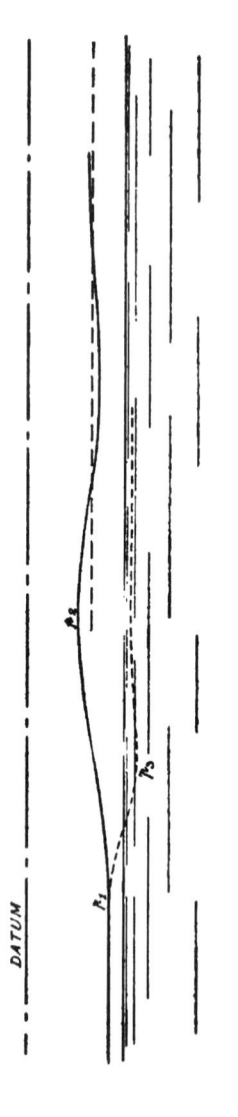

Fig 15.

PLATE VIII.

"FLYING BOAT" TYPE.
Built by Messrs. WHITE & THOMPSON.

PLATE IX.

HYDRO-AEROPLANE H.R.E.3. *R.A.F. Design for the "Naval Wing" (Now R.N. Air Service) in 1912.*

AEROPLANE AND SUBMARINE.   § 73

experience. The path of the torpedo is indicated by the dotted line p, p_1. It is even possible to diminish the disturbance still further by arranging the torpedo somewhat behind the position above assumed, so that on discharge the centre of gravity moves forward. This would in some degree compensate for the loss of weight as giving a less net change in the natural velocity. In the opinion of the author, however, it is not to be recommended, since it would result in the machine being catastrophically unstable (prior to the discharge of the torpedo), or would at least tend in that direction.

§ 74. *Aeroplane and Submarine.* It is well known that the submarine, although when submerged invisible to an observer or "look-out" on the deck of a warship or other vessel, is clearly visible, and may be readily located by an aeronaut from a sufficient altitude. The conditions are similar to those frequently noticed when fish in a river are seen clearly from a bridge, but are invisible from the river-bank. The torpedo-boat or destroyer when operating against the submarine is at a considerable disadvantage, inasmuch as when the latter is submerged the only visible sign of its presence is its periscope—a pole of a few inches in diameter, projecting some few feet out of the water. Ordinarily it is the point where the periscope "rips" the surface that forms the most conspicuous visible indication. Thus we may anticipate that, in the future, operations directed against the submarines of an enemy will involve the employment of aircraft, at least as a means of reconnaissance. It is an important fact that in this particular service the enemy (the submarine) has no power of offence; hence it is possible that the dirigible may prove itself as well suited to the work as the aeroplane. It is true that the modern submarine is being fitted with guns of light calibre, but these are only available after the vessel has come to

Fig. 16.

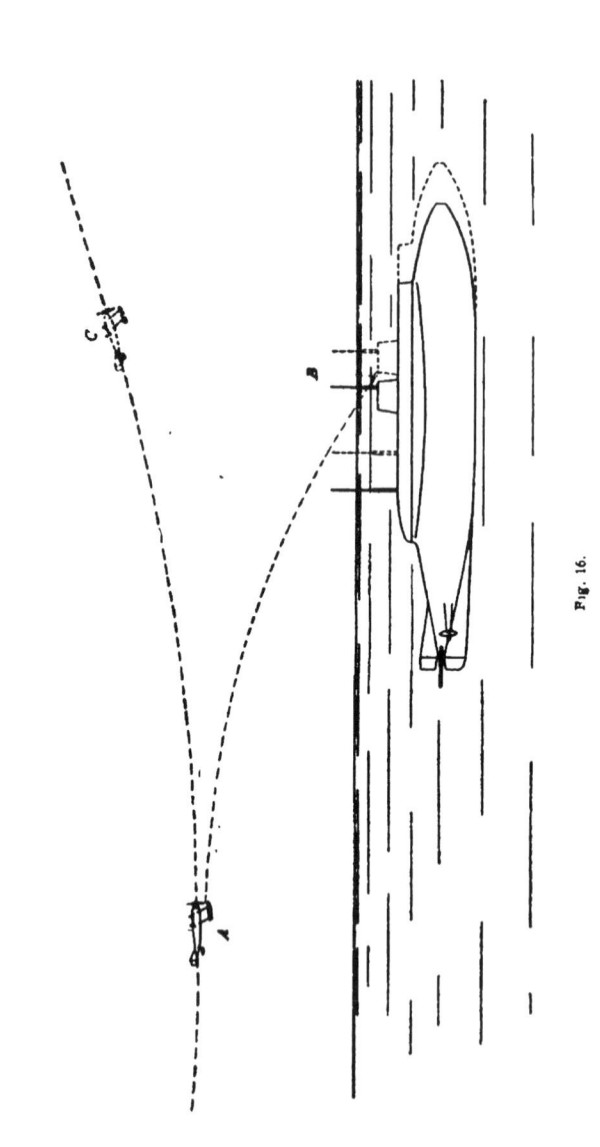

AEROPLANE AND SUBMARINE. § 74

the surface. We may presume that in any operations of the description contemplated, one or more destroyers or light cruisers will accompany the aircraft scout, and the conning-tower of the submarine will be blown away within a few seconds of its appearance.

§ 75. *Attack on Submarine by Aeroplane. Destruction by Bomb.* It is not in any sense certain or likely that the operations of aircraft in relation to the submarine will be confined to observation. In the opinion of the author, aircraft, whether aeroplane or dirigible, will prove to be the submarine's most dangerous enemy, the submarine being attacked by bombs charged with high explosive while submerged. Owing to the absence of any danger of counter-attack the aeroplane may fly as low as deemed desirable to obtain the necessary accuracy of aim, and much of the difficulty commonly associated with bomb-dropping will accordingly vanish. Such an attack is depicted (somewhat diagrammatically) in Fig. 16, in which, for the purpose of illustration, the machine is shown as flying at a quite low altitude of about 60 ft., and when at the point A to drop a bomb, which, having the velocity of the machine in flight, describes the trajectory A B whilst the machine is travelling to the point C; the motion of the submarine in the intervening time is indicated by the dotted outline. It is not to be anticipated that in practice it will be found necessary to come down to as low an altitude as that shown in order to ensure the degree of accuracy required.

The type of bomb appropriate to the duty in question, although not greatly different from that required in connection with land service, will need a certain amount of consideration. In view of the fact that the size of the hole blown in the skin of the submarine is not important, the charge of explosive may be quite moderate; probably 10 lb. or 15 lb. of wet gun-

§ 75 AIRCRAFT IN WARFARE.

cotton will be ample. A bomb of torpedo-like form, about 6 in. in diameter, and fitted with a sheet-metal cruciform tail, as shown diagrammatically in Fig. 17, would probably be found suitable; it would be furnished with a positive impact or contact fuse at its nose. The usual way of dropping a bomb of this type is broadside on, pointing in the direction of flight; the axis then remains tangent to the trajectory throughout the fall, the tail acting in the manner of the feathering of an arrow.

A bomb of the type described in the preceding paragraph will travel through water under the influence of gravity at a no inconsiderable velocity. Taking its weight to be (immersed) about half a hundredweight, its limiting velocity in water will be about 50 ft. per second,

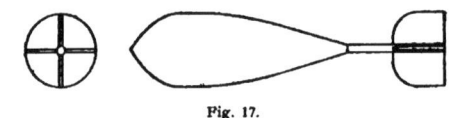

Fig. 17.

which is ample to ensure the certain action of the contact fuse. Thus it will be impossible for a submarine to escape by deep immersion, presuming it to remain sufficiently visible to permit of attack.

§ 76. *Submarine Activity as Affected by Aircraft.* In brief, the aeroplane, and to some degree other aircraft, suitably armed, may be expected to prove an effective check on the unbridled activity of the submarine. With a properly-equipped naval aeroplane service, supported by a few fast, light cruisers, such as the type known as the "destroyer leader," the enemy's submarines will be unable to roam at large or to make unexpected attacks on our cruiser patrols. They will need to operate under the protection of a supporting force, and will only leave that

AEROPLANE AND SUBMARINE. § 76

protection at the risk of almost certain destruction. Or they will require to confine their activities to raiding by night—a form of activity in which their radius of action is essentially limited, and, save under exceptional circumstances, of doubtful promise. It must not be assumed, however, that the service necessary for the effective patrolling of the seas by aeroplane will prove at all a simple or easy matter. The provision of the needed bases, coastal and floating, alone will be a formidable matter, and as the radius of action of the submarine is increased, and the field of operations is thereby widened, the work will become more and more arduous. Again, the enemy's aircraft will always have to be reckoned with.

Thus, although the air service may be looked to to provide an effective limit to the power of the submarine, we can never expect or anticipate that the value or utility of the latter will be by any means nullified.

CHAPTER XII.
(November 20th, 1914).

THE NAVAL AIR-SCOUT. THE FLYING-BOAT TYPE. THE DOUBLE FLOAT TYPE. THE OCEAN-GOING FLOATING BASE OR PONTOON SHIP.

§ 77. *The Duties of Naval Reconnaissance.* The work of scouting, or reconnaissance, will undoubtedly be the first and most important duty of aircraft in the service of the Navy. Whether it be in connection with the work of coast defence, in giving timely warning of the approach of hostile vessels of war, or in searching out and reporting the whereabouts of an enemy's battle fleet, in locating the enemy's commerce-destroyers on the high seas, or in directing gun-fire during a bombardment or a fleet action, the employment of aircraft cannot fail to be of signal value.

So far as coastal work is concerned, there appears to be no present difficulty in effectually patrolling the whole of the home waters to a distance of some 200 or 300 miles from our shores, other than the want of the necessary machines and the requisite organisation—that is to say, there is no difficulty of a technical or engineering character. To some extent, as touching more especially points of strategic importance, aircraft are already occupied in this duty; the extension of the system is mainly a matter of increase in materiel and personnel. Unfortunately the demand and pressure for increase are felt in all branches of the aeronautical services, and it cannot but take some considerable time to build additional machines, apart from the time which

AIRCRAFT AND NAVAL RECONNAISSANCE. § 77

must be expended in the training of the personnel and in accumulating the experience necessary to determine what types and establishment are really necessary.

§ 78. *Type of Aircraft as imposed by Extraneous Conditions.* In connection with the work of reconnaissance in home waters, where the "base" is a station situated on or in the region of a coast-line, it is well understood that the length and extent of the coast-line is a matter of considerable importance. If, on the one hand, the base be situated on a small island or promontory in the vicinity of hostile or neutral country, a dirigible or other similar low-velocity machine is clearly unsuitable. In the event of a 'high wind it would frequently be impossible for it to return to its base; tersely, it would be blown away. If, on the other hand, the base be situated on a long stretch of coast-line (such as the East Coast of Great Britain) with a number of well-placed stations, the risk is comparatively small; since, unless the wind is directly off shore (or nearly so) it will always be possible to make some other "port" than that of origin; the chance of its being lost will be remote.

When the operations in contemplation are far removed from home, beyond the radius of action of aeroplanes operating from a coast station or from friendly territory, we find ourselves confronted with difficulties of a kind for which there is no parallel in land operations. As pointed out in the preceding chapter, two solutions are possible. Either the machine must be capable of alighting on, and rising from, the water, and of riding in safety on the surface of the sea or ocean under ordinary weather conditions, and so be able to accompany and act as an auxiliary to a warship or squadron at sea; or some kind of sea-going pontoon vessel must be devised from which machines can be launched and on whose deck they may alight. Both these schemes are evidently practicable, and each has its advantages and difficulties.

§ 79. *Advantages of Flying-Boat Type.* For the former scheme the most suitable type of machine would appear to be the "flying boat"—that is to say, the type in which the flotation, when riding at anchor, is derived from a hull of boat shape and of seaworthy design, with the usual "hydroplane" stepped bottom to give the necessary lift to cause the craft to rise on the water and skim whilst acquiring the speed necessary for flight. It is by no means certain that this single hull or boat will oust the double float at present more generally adopted, but for the larger naval aircraft, weighing probably upwards of two or three tons, the single boat may be reasonably expected to prove the more seaworthy, especially in heavy weather. In discussing the question recently[*] the author made the suggestion that, for the sea-going aeroplane (such as now under discussion), it may be found advantageous to make arrangements for the abandonment of the flight organs, and to provide a marine propeller, so that in case of emergency the hull may be navigated as an ordinary motor-boat. The flying boat will thus, it is anticipated, be found the most convenient type of machine to act as sea-going air-scout to the cruiser or battleship. It is a type which may be so designed as to be readily stripped and carried in davits, the flight organs being fitted, and the boat otherwise made ready for air service, when required. For the commerce-raider, or the cruiser or cruiser squadron detailed for the destruction of the hostile commerce-raider, an air-scout capable of being carried in this manner would prove of the greatest value. In really bad weather it would not perhaps be possible to launch or fly a machine of this type; but so far as present experience

[*] James Forrest Lecture, Institution of Civil Engineers, 1914.

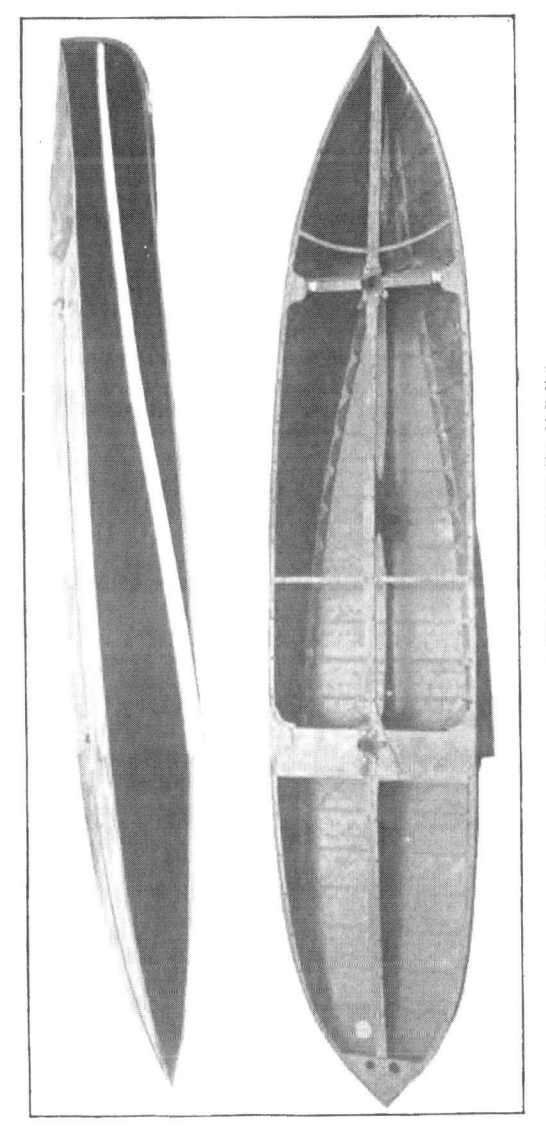

FLOATS, 1912 TYPE, AS FITTED TO H.R.E.3.
Compare Plate IX.

DOUBLE-FLOAT AND FLYING-BOAT TYPES. § 79

goes, it is impossible to fly any aeroplane which has to rise from the water under such conditions. However, if it should prove possible to fly, as an average, on but half the total days in the year, the extended range of vision obtained (even by such limited use of the air scout) would frequently prove of decisive value. In the case, for example, of the recent pursuit of the Emden and Königsberg, if our cruisers had been able to sweep a belt of some 200 or 300 miles in width (instead of about one-tenth of that amount), the result might have been achieved in far less time. A cruiser, well served by its air scouts, in pursuit of an enemy (if not fast enough or strong enough to give battle), would be able, having located the enemy, to warn merchantmen of their danger and at the same time to call for the requisite reinforcements. It would also be no longer possible for an enemy cruiser to secure concealment amongst the islands of an archipelago or in a river mouth or estuary.

§ 80. *Points in Favour of the Double-Float.* For the duties of bomb and torpedo air-craft, discussed in detail in the preceding chapter, the boat type of machine is ill-suited; the conditions are such as would indicate the two-float type as necessary. The latter admits of the bomb-magazine or torpedo-cradle being arranged centrally beneath the fuselage, from which position, by suitable release mechanism, the missile or torpedo can be readily let fall. It is doubtful, on the other hand, whether the two-float type will prove as convenient to handle aboard a vessel not especially fitted out for its reception, and it is further doubtful whether it will prove as seaworthy when compelled to depend on its own resources. However, there are authorities who are disposed even to give it preference on the latter count, and certainly for the smaller craft there is something to be said in favour of the fact that, so long as the floats are intact and

§ 80   AIRCRAFT IN WARFARE.

uninjured, the machine is virtually unsinkable—it cannot be swamped, as is the case with the boat-type.

A serious disadvantage under which the sea-going aeroplane at present labours, whether it be of the single boat or double-float type, is that its speed is essentially limited by the fact that it has to alight and take off from the water, and this involves designing to a comparatively low minimum flight velocity. Whilst not necessarily limiting the mean or maximum in like degree it tends in that direction.

§ 81. *The Ocean-Going Aeroplane Pontoon Base or Pontoon Ship.* Passing now to the alternative scheme—the aeroplane pontoon-ship, we find opened up possibilities of quite a different kind. We are no longer concerned *of necessity* with the limitations imposed by rising from or alighting on water, and the vessel will be expressly designed to suit the aeroplane service, instead of the aeroplane requiring to adapt itself to the vessel. Any land type of machine could be used from the pontoon-ship, but by preference floats would be fitted, and so far as practicable, machines would be rendered amphibious. Whilst it is evidently desirable that all machines in the service of the Navy should be able to rise from the sea, the conditions are evidently altered when an immersion is to be regarded as an accident rather than as part of the regular routine.

For the primary function of the aeronautical arm in the Navy, whether it be scouting, or attack on the submarine, or torpedo work, there is no outstanding advantage in the employment of machines in great numbers. For the latter duty (when the machine for this class of work has been developed), it may be found desirable to attack by squadrons or flights rather than by individual machines. But even this is doubtful, since the advantage gained by simultaneous attack from different points of

THE FLOATING BASE OR PONTOON-SHIP. § 81

the compass, as preventing the enemy from concentrating his fire on any one machine, may be more than outweighed by the greater risk of the impending attack being detected and reported by the enemy's air service or torpedo craft. When, however, we have to consider the demands which will be made on the naval air-service for the performance of its secondary function, in addition to the occasions when it will be required to act in connection with land operations, it is evident that provision must be made for transporting and handling machines in large numbers, and this, so far as can be made practicable, irrespective of ordinarily bad weather conditions, and independently of any land station or base. It is here that the need for the floating base or pontoon-ship will be felt.

We may anticipate that, apart from such mechanical detail as alighting gear, relative petrol capacity, etc., the requirements of the naval and military machines for the destruction of hostile aircraft will not differ greatly. Each will rely mainly on the gun in some shape or form for its power of offence, and will depend upon its speed to force the enemy into engagement. Both types will be sent into action in the greatest numerical strength that circumstances permit, or as limited by the number that can be handled or manœuvred without undue danger to themselves, in order to bring the heaviest fire concentration upon the enemy, and to take full advantage of the *n-square* law. To this end the whole subject of *formation flying* will need to be studied exhaustively and practised assiduously both in time of peace and in time of war. For the time being, however, we are concerned with the question of the floating base—whose object is to render it possible to mobilise an air fleet, as contemplated (complete with repair depôt and supplies of every kind) at any point required, in the shortest possible space of time.

§ 82   AIRCRAFT IN WARFARE.

§ 82. *Conditions to be fulfilled*. The conditions which it is desirable that the air-service pontoon-ship shall fill are, briefly, as follow :—

(1) To act as storage and transport for a fleet of *at least* three squadrons, say fifty or sixty machines, complete with spares, fuel and oil supplies, and personnel, together with all guns, ammunition, bombs, torpedoes, etc., necessary for complete equipment.

(2) To carry a workshop fully equipped, together with the necessary mechanical staff to deal with repairs, etc., such as are reasonably required to maintain the said air fleet in fighting order.

(3) To provide an upper deck of sufficient area to act as an "alighting ground" completely free from obstruction—*i.e.*, there may be no masts, funnels, ventilators, cranes, searchlight platform, or wireless apparatus such as would form a permanent projection above the flying-deck level. The conditions as to deck area, etc., must be such as to give ample room for alighting or getting off to a pilot of ordinary skill.

(4) It must have a speed exceeding 20 knots in order that it may be able to accompany a battle fleet at sea, or to render it able to save itself by flight from an enemy battle squadron.

(5) It must have a gun armament of sufficient power to protect it from attack by the light fast cruisers of the enemy.

(6) It must be of comparatively shallow draught, as light as is consistent with its sea-going qualities and other requirements, in order that it may be able to act in rivers, harbours, or estuary regions in support of land operations, and incidentally to enable it to evade pursuit and destruction by war vessels of heavy draught and gun power (such as the battle-cruiser) by taking refuge in shoal water.

THE FLOATING BASE OR PONTOON-SHIP. § 83

§ 83. *The Pontoon-Ship, Specification.* The above list of requirements indicate at once that the pontoon vessel will need to be a ship of very large size, comparable to that of a first-class battleship, at least as to length and beam. Beyond this, taking the requirements in order, there appears to be nothing really difficult or impossible of fulfilment. Thus, conditions (1) and (2) could be met without difficulty by a specially-designed vessel of a few thousand tons displacement. Condition (3) is more exacting, and requires that the vessel should be of the maximum beam admissible—say 90 ft.—with a water-line of not less than 500 ft.; also the need for doing away with funnels probably means that the internal-combustion engine will have to be considered as the means of propulsion. This, for the horse-power required—about 15,000 indicated—is rather beyond anything yet attempted; however, it can be by no means deemed impossible. The conditions could be met by employing six propeller-shafts, each driven by a Diesel unit of 2,500 indicated horse-power; this is not regarded as by any means beyond the limits of commercially sound engineering. The present day uses of the *masts* of a warship are mainly for signalling (by wireless and otherwise), to serve to carry searchlight and lookout platforms, and as an anchorage for jib-cranes. All these various requirements will need to be met without hampering the flying-deck with any permanent obstructions. Thus it is well understood that the "aerial" for a wireless installation may be arranged horizontally; in the present case it could be carried on spar outriggers, some 10 ft. or 15 ft. away from the gunwale, being shipped and unshipped as needed. Searchlights could, without difficulty, be mounted on telescopic pillars dropping flush into the deck, operated by hydraulic power or other means, and taking but a few seconds to raise or lower;

§ 83   AIRCRAFT IN WARFARE.

cranes also can be provided in such form as to be rigged only when needed. Altogether there is nothing in these detail requirements likely to prove of insuperable difficulty. Condition (5) would be adequately met by a powerful broadside armament of 6-in. guns, in addition, perhaps, to guns of heavier calibre mounted in a single turret astern, all arranged below the level of the flying-deck. With a ship of the size contemplated there should be no difficulty in providing a sufficient weight of armament for the purpose specified. The gun-deck would be the main upper structural deck of the vessel, with only the comparatively light flying-deck above it.

§ 84. *Advantage of Pontoon-Ship as Aeroplane Base.* The pontoon-ship as an aeroplane base possesses certain and obvious disadvantages; an area for alighting such as is presented by the deck of a ship, although it may be, say, 90 ft. beam by 400 ft. or more in length, is none too large under really bad conditions of weather for even a skilled pilot, especially if the vessel be rolling in a heavy seaway. Without doubt, under extreme conditions operations will become frankly impossible; but, under similar conditions, it will be also impossible to employ a machine designed to rise from the water. The conditions in the case of the pontoon-ship, however, are not really so unfavourable as might be thought; the vessel can always be brought head to wind, when the relative velocity of the machine on alighting will be reduced by the velocity of the wind; it may also be still further reduced by maintaining the vessel under power; these two effects in combination, assuming the wind to be 40 miles per hour and the vessel at full speed, will result in a machine, flying through the air at 60 miles per hour, taking the deck without any relative motion whatever—a most favourable state of things, permitting

THE FLOATING BASE OR PONTOON-SHIP. § 84

it to be instantly secured and made fast. Beyond this, under the said condition—*i.e.*, head to wind—it is only in the exceptional case of a heavy cross sea that the rolling could be serious, and with the modern methods of steadying sea-going vessels (gyroscopes and ballast-tanks) it would require a quite exceptional state of weather to keep the air fleet imprisoned. There is one constructional point worthy of mention; the flying-deck will require to "run-out" at the bows of the ship in easy lines, to avoid setting up eddies or dead regions, such as might affect the stability or buoyancy of machines landing or leaving the deck; to some extent it may be found necessary to extend this precaution to where deck joins gunwale abeam.

It is also worthy of note that the proposed pontoon-ship, being of comparatively light draught and great beam, will possess naturally the type of stability of a raft rather than that of an ordinary ocean-going vessel, and will thus tend in a seaway to follow the changing slope and motion of the long ocean waves. Now this slope and motion, as is well known, are so co-ordinated that the normal to the wave slope is always the *apparent plumb*, and so it may even turn out that the flying-machine, on taking the deck of a vessel studied as a raft rather than as a ship, will (even when the motion is severe) have no tendency either to side-slip overboard or turn turtle.

The same conditions which are favourable to alighting, as from the point of view of relative motion, are also favourable to the machine when getting away. Thus, with a 40-mile-per-hour wind and a vessel at full speed, head to wind (as already assumed), a machine will be able to leave the deck with a relative motion of only some 10 or 20 miles per hour and a flight velocity of 70 or 80 miles per hour. Taking all the possibilities of the

§ 84   AIRCRAFT IN WARFARE.

situation into account, it is probable that the machines to operate from a pontoon will, on the whole, be constructed as faster fliers than those designed for rising from the water, and to that extent at least will be better fitted for combatant duties.

PLATE XI.

R.A.F. TYPE R.E.1 (1912) FOLDED FOR TRANSPORT OR STORAGE.

CHAPTER XIII.
(November 27th, 1914).

THE COMMAND OF THE AIR.

§ 85. *Air Power as Affecting Combined Tactics.* Some indication has been given in the preceding articles of the influence that the advent of aircraft may be expected to have on the tactical value and employment of the other Arms of the Services; more particularly attention has been called to the changes that will almost inevitably be found necessary in the employment of cavalry. Certain writers, basing their views too exclusively on the experience of the present war, have expressed the opinion that the aeroplane, and, more broadly, aircraft, though of the greatest service and utility as a new means of reconnaissance (and, to some extent, of offence), will not have any material influence on the tactical employment of the older Arms, either Infantry, Cavalry, or Artillery. In the opinion of the author this view is fallacious, and the present war, at least so far as developed, cannot be taken as a criterion. It may be thought overbold thus to give preference to purely theoretical deduction in place of actual experience, but a little consideration will show that the experience, such as it is, cannot be regarded as a serious indication of the future. It is an undeniable fact that the aeroplane has, in the present war, been able to give information of the positions and movements of the enemy such as would have been otherwise unobtainable, and in a few cases it has enabled points to be attacked which could not have

§ 85 AIRCRAFT IN WARFARE.

been reached by any other means. To this extent it may be said to have invented or originated new duties not overlapping those of the older Arms. It is equally true that, so far, it has not seriously encroached by its employment on the duties of the other Arms—it has not replaced cavalry in any measurable degree, neither has aeroplane bombardment been found effective as a substitute for gun-fire. There is, however, one important consideration that should prevent us from drawing too hasty a conclusion from these facts. The number of aeroplanes at present in service (as already pointed out) is small in comparison with the size of the armies in the field, so much so that we can only afford to employ our aeroplanes for work for which they are pre-eminently suited; that is to say, to perform mainly those duties which cannot be done by other means.

The position is perhaps most easily illustrated by means of an analogy. Some years ago, when the milling-machine was first introduced into our general engineering shops, it was not an uncommon thing to see one such machine installed (more or less experimentally) in a large machine-shop alongside some hundred or so lathes and other machine-tools; such a machine usually had allotted to it a number of odd jobs that could not be done conveniently or cheaply on any other machine. Any superficial observer asked to report on the innovation might have been tempted to say, "By means of this new machine work may be undertaken which could not, commercially speaking, be done previously; it does not, however, show any promise of replacing to any extent the older forms of machine-tool, and can only be regarded as useful for doing the special work for which it has shown itself of unique value." Such a view would, we know, have been utterly wrong. The milling-machine to-day is doing a multitude of jobs formerly looked upon

INFLUENCE ON COMBINED TACTICS.   § 86

as essentially work for the lathe or planing-machine, but *it had no opportunity of demonstrating its full capacity until installed in sufficient numbers.* The above is merely an illustration chosen from innumerable examples which might be cited.

§ 86. *General Influence on Combined Tactics. Aircraft as affecting Attack and Defence.* Without attempting to discuss fully the influence of the development of the Fourth Arm on questions of "grand" or "combined" tactics, mention may be made of one salient fact which has already become manifest; the influence of aircraft as a means of reconnaissance has greatly increased the power of *defence* without, it would appear, conferring a commensurate benefit on the *attack.* It is possible that the fighting power of the aeroplane may in the future be found to redress the balance of advantages; but, so far, there is no definite indication that this will be the case.

It may be stated tersely that the equilibrium between forces conducting respectively an attack and defence is normally maintained by a balance between strategic and tactical advantages. Thus the tactical advantage lies with the defender, in so far that he may be presumed to occupy chosen positions carefully prepared and fortified in advance, so that to place the attack on terms of equality the force employed must (locally at least) be numerically stronger; a numerical superiority many times that of the defending force may be required. The strategic advantage is with the attacking force, owing to the fact that the general in command can select any one of a number of possible points at which to deliver his assault. By exerting pressure at other points, by way of feint, he can keep the enemy in ignorance of his intentions whilst he is concentrating at the point chosen for the main attack, and so prevent him (the defender)

§ 86   AIRCRAFT IN WARFARE.

taking steps to reinforce his lines. Thus an attacking army can always ensure a local numerical superiority at the decisive moment, and the issue will largely depend on whether this advantage is sufficient to outweigh the tactical advantage of the defending force as due to its choice of position and entrenchments and other defensive works. Clearly much, if not everything, depends upon the general in command of the attack being able successfully to conceal his movements until the moment arrives for delivering his blow. But the veil of secrecy has been lifted by the advent of aircraft. It is for this reason that the power of aerial reconnaissance has proved so valuable a weapon to the defending force, and of comparatively little value to the attack. It is quite true that the aircraft of the attacking force may be of considerable use in reporting the nature and strength of the defences, and so may disclose the points of weakness at which the chances of successful assault are the greatest: but this will only in a very small degree compensate for the premature disclosure of the whole plan of attack to the defenders, a disclosure which, if we may judge from experience so far gained, appears to be little short of complete.

The foregoing applies more particularly to warfare in which large bodies of troops are engaged over a great extent of territory; evidently where fighting is on a small scale, and the whole of the movement constituting a concentration and attack can be executed between sunset and sunrise, the operations can be considered to be of a purely tactical character. It may be emphasised that it is by destroying the *strategic advantage* hitherto enjoyed by the attack that aeronautical reconnaissance gains its especial value as an aid to the defence. Thus, so far, the advent of aircraft in the field of battle has had the effect of tending to produce a deadlock, or position of stalemate, such as we are able to witness at the present time in the north-west of France and on the Belgian frontier.

§ 87. *Previous Improvements in Weapons and Armament. Question of Depth of Fighting Line.* It is of interest to note that, previously to the arrival of the aeroplane, most of the improvements of weapons and armament have tended to favour the attack and to render defence more difficult. During the last three or four centuries we have seen the value of permanent defences gradually diminish, as constructional improvements and scientific methods of usage have rendered the Artillery Arm more and more deadly. Of more recent times we have witnessed the result of the increased effectiveness of fire-arms generally in the greater concentration that can be effected on any given point in a field of battle. In other words, the *depth* of the line has been increased by the greater range of small-arms, and it may to-day be increased almost indefinitely by the employment of artillery of heavier and heavier calibre, with correspondingly increased range. Such increase in the depth of the line only becomes of general value when, as in the present war, the number of men per mile of front is great, and more men are available than can be effectively employed in the trenches or infantry supports. Any additional numerical strength must then be assigned to the Artillery Arm, and the greater the supply of men (in other words, the greater the density of the line), the greater becomes the relative importance of Artillery: then the heavier and longer range should be the artillery brought into action, in order to ensure that the weight of numbers shall tell, in some degree at least, in accordance with the *n-square* law. It would seem that this is a point which has been very fully realised by the German Staff. In our own experience it is certain that the Boer War, owing to the comparative openness of the country

§ 87   AIRCRAFT IN WARFARE.

and less density of the fighting-line, did not fully demonstrate the importance of artillery from the standpoint of modern European warfare.

§ 88. *The Command of the Air.* It is probable that in the future the employment of aircraft in large numbers, tactically in a combative capacity, may, in effect, still further deepen the fighting-line. Without attempting to predict exactly what *rôle* the aeroplane will take in this regard, it is safe to say that if, during a battle, it is found practicable to conduct air raids and air attacks systematically over a considerable belt of territory in the rear of an enemy's lines, this belt will require to be defended, and (if the air forces employed are of numerical strength comparable to the other Arms) the belt will actually become a measure of the depth of front. The permanent defeat of the enemy's air fleet and, as we may express it, the *capture of his air* will then become the first and most important duty of the Aeronautical Arm. It is difficult to gauge what the total consequence of defeating the enemy in the air will be. It is unlikely that it will entirely prevent his aerial reconnaissance; his scouts will doubtless manage to run the gauntlet and continue to keep him sufficiently informed. On the other hand, he will be deprived of all those uses of the Aeronautical Arm in which some more direct and definite purpose is involved, such as the direction of gun-fire, defence of stores, protection of cavalry, etc. He will require to submit to aeroplane attack without possibility of effective counter; he will be subjected to long-range gun-fire (directed by aeroplane) without means of returning it; his cavalry will be continually harassed by machine-gun fire and explosive grenades, and will cease to be of service; his railways, convoys, and mechanical transport will be nowhere safe; and he will need to expend an undue proportion of his resources in patrolling his lines of communication and guarding points of strategic importance. The command of the air opens up possibilities in the direction of raiding of a kind and with a scope not hitherto known in warfare. To what extent it will be found possible for aircraft to detach themselves from their base, and execute extended raids in territory held by the enemy, only the future can determine. It would certainly appear that if the inhabitants are friendly, and the enemy's aircraft are no more a force to be reckoned with, tactics of this kind may be quite feasible.

Once again the author would point out that the experience of the present war is no guide; the Aeronautical Arm *quâ* Arm cannot at present be said to exist. The Flying Corps, excellent though it be, is scarcely more than necessary to constitute an armed reconnaissance service.

§ 89. *Total Defeat in the Air an Irreparable Disaster.* From the foregoing it would appear to be at least doubtful whether in future warfare an army which has been deprived of its aircraft, or has to admit the air supremacy of an enemy, will find itself in a position to carry on a campaign. It is, in any case, certain that it will only be able to do so at a very grave disadvantage. It is the author's opinion that the time will come when the total and irretrievable loss of the command of the air to an enemy will be regarded as a disaster of an altogether irreparable and decisive kind, and although there may be a great deal of fighting still before the end, nothing less than an overwhelming superiority in the other arms will save an army deprived of its air service from ultimate defeat. We are thus led to the consideration of a branch of the subject of extreme importance— namely, *aeroplane tactics.*

§ 90. *Employment of Aircraft in Large Bodies. Air Tactics.* In some of the previous Chapters (Chapter

§ 90   AIRCRAFT IN WARFARE.

VII., *et seq.*) the question of aircraft fighting—*i.e.*, aeroplane *versus* aeroplane—has been considered, and matters such as armament have been fully discussed. We shall now deal with the employment of the armed machine in its fighting capacity, not as a single unit, but as part of a force whose function is the destruction of the armed air fleet of the enemy, and the crippling of his reconnaissance service. It is evidently necessary to assume that the enemy in his turn has prepared an armed air fleet, and that the problem to be studied is the handling and bringing to battle of the two air fleets in their struggle for supremacy.

The various factors that enter into the problem, apart from the personnel are those of speed, climbing power, armament, and last, but not least, numerical strength. These, together with that all-important item—the tactical scheme—are the more weighty of the material factors on which the question of victory or defeat will turn. The relative importance of the different items is not by any means always the same. It may, for example, usually be assumed that one or the other of the combatant forces is seeking, and the other endeavouring to avoid, battle, or at least is only willing to accept battle under conditions deemed favourable; thus it may be that the enemy can be only brought to battle by virtue of superior speed. In other cases it will be possible to force the enemy to give battle by attack upon some vulnerable point connected with his land forces; all this is strictly analogous to the similar problems of naval warfare. Given the main conditions, all that can be accomplished by a tactical scheme is to ensure engaging the enemy in the most favourable manner possible, and, as in the problems studied in Chapters V. and VI., bringing the greatest weight of numbers possible to bear on lesser numbers of the enemy, in order to reap the advantage of the *n-square* law. The object of the practice of tactical exercises will be to enable an air fleet to manœuvre to defeat the enemy in detail, and, if his numbers are superior, to prevent him from bringing his whole concentrated fire to bear by the adroit handling of the weaker numbers, and so to neutralise the advantage of his numerically superior force.

CHAPTER XIV.
(December 4th, 1914).

AN INDEPENDENT AIR FLEET AND ITS DUTIES. AIR TACTICS AND FORMATION FLYING. AIR AND NAVAL TACTICS: CONDITIONS COMPARED.

§ 91. *Need for an Independent Combatant Air Fleet.* The subject of aeroplane tactics, or air tactics, may be said to lie wholly with the future. Hitherto the aeroplane has acted in its combative capacity as an individual unit; there has been no systematic co-operation between a number of machines for the organised destruction of the enemy aircraft, such as could be described as tactics in the military sense.

Before we can usefully discuss the present branch of the subject we must look forward to the time when air fleets or squadrons will be organised for the purpose of operating together according to some well-understood, or prearranged, scheme as combatant units. We have already defined the duties of attack and defence by air against the air forces of the enemy as constituting the secondary function of the Aeronautical Arm. This being the mainspring from which the tactics of the air must derive its motive, we require to take for our foundation the material provided by our previous consideration of the primary function of the Arm.

The initial condition of the problem, then, is that both combatant armies are provided with reconnaissance machines of two types, namely, the long-distance or strategic scout—an unarmed machine built for speed and endurance, and the tactical scout, probably mounting a

AN INDEPENDENT AIR FLEET. § 91

machine-gun, and protected by light armour from attack from below. Possibly also there will be a type more especially designed for lending support to ordinary military operations, on the lines already foreshadowed, protected beneath by heavier armour or by point-blank-proof shields, and mounting a multiple machine-gun, or a mitrailleuse having three or four barrels, and capable of firing 2,000 to 3,000 rounds per minute. Further than this, there will without doubt be machines expressly constructed for bomb-dropping, in addition to specialised naval types; these, however, do not require particular consideration, since, in view of the weight they have otherwise to carry, their power of offence against hostile aircraft (as measured by their gun-power) will of necessity be feeble.

In the absence of any organised air fleet intended for the destruction of the types as above defined, there will take place, indeed as is already the case, a certain amount of desultory fighting of a local character; at one point the aircraft of one belligerent will secure the advantage, and at some other point the reverse may be the case. So long as neither air force possesses any marked superiority in the matter of speed, and so long as neither army has at its disposal more machines than are reasonably necessary for the reconnaissance and other services mentioned, we cannot anticipate that the results of such aerial combat will be decisive in any sense. We may assume that numbers may combine in order to overweight the enemy locally, and drive him out of action; the advantage obtained, however, will only be temporary. In such desultory air warfare there will be a continual wastage of men and machines, but these losses can be made good by new units and new formations.

In order to effect anything decisive, an organisation of an entirely new character is required: an air fleet absolutely free from any routine or other set duties, whose one and only object is to seek out the enemy's aircraft wherever reported, and effect their destruction with the utmost swiftness and despatch; in brief, an independent air fleet, whose unchallenged existence alone stands for the command of the air.

§ 92. *The Independent Air Fleet. Air Tactics.* It may be laid down that the independent air fleet, in order that it shall be capable of fulfilling the duties assigned to it, must be strong by virtue of numbers. In order to destroy—*i.e.*, not merely to drive away—the active aircraft of the enemy, it must be of decisively higher speed, so that the enemy, whether reconnaissance or fighting machines, will be compelled to surrender or give battle. An exception may be made in the case of the strategic scout, which, being designed purely for speed and being burdened with neither armour or armament, may be taken as, within reason, faster than anything that can be brought against it. This need for superiority in the matter of speed means evidently that the air-fleet type must suffer in some degree in the matter of armament; alternatively it must be a heavier type machine for machine. Closely allied to the question of speed is that of climbing power. Other things being equal, whether for increased speed or for increased climbing power, a greater horse-power per unit weight is necessary. If we assume some given value for the horse-power per unit weight, then a machine may be designed either to develop the highest flight speed possible or to obtain the greatest rate of altitude increase—*i.e.*, vertical velocity. Any actual design is of the nature of a compromise; maximum flight speed is kept as high as possible consistently with obtaining a sufficient rapidity of ascent. The independent air fleet must be, without question, the master of the service machines whose

AIR TACTICS. THE UPPER "GAGE."   § 92

destruction it is required to encompass, both in the matter of speed and climbing capacity. Thus it will require to possess a considerable superiority in the essential matter of horse-power; it must be made impossible for its prey to escape either by horizontal flight or by putting on altitude.*

§ 93. *Tactical Importance of Altitude.* This question of altitude is one of really vital consequence in connection with the tactics of the air. The service machine designed to fulfil the primary function of the Arm must evidently carry its protective plating or armour distributed in such manner as best to resist gun-fire from below. Also the armament is necessarily directed mainly to the downward projection of missiles, by gun-fire or otherwise. Hence to obtain the "upper berth" in an air-fleet action is at the outset to secure a great tactical advantage. It might be supposed that these considerations will lead to an increase in the protection accorded—that is to say, that the service fighting-machine will be fitted with a complete panoply of steel plate, above as well as below. This, however, is improbable, since any such measure would, by reason of the additional weight, so reduce the general mobility of the machine as to constitute too serious a handicap. It would appear to be only possible to ameliorate the conditions under which a machine will have to fight when resisting an attack from above by arranging the gun armament with as great a capacity for upward fire as possible. A further advantage in the possession of the upper berth or "gage" lies in the fact that the potential energy, represented by the difference of altitude, may, at any time, be used to augment the velocity of flight

* Perhaps the above is asking too much. When a fleet is of sufficient numerical strength it may be that a definite superiority in climbing power will not be necessary. Thus sections of the fleet may be told off to operate at various different altitudes, so that escape from one section will mean engagement by another. If the *choice of altitude* is thus left to the enemy, it is clear that the numerical superiority will need to be overwhelming.

137

§ 93   AIRCRAFT IN WARFARE.

above normal, a power which cannot fail to be of real tactical value.

§ 94. *Air Fleet must be Homogeneous.* It is a fact which cannot be too strongly stated that the independent air fleet must be homogeneous. It must be composed of units of approximately the same capacity of speed and climbing power; the range of its weapons also should be the same. As a counsel of perfection, the fleet should be of *one design*, mounting one standard type of gun, using one kind of ammunition. Owing to the need for aeronautical ascendancy, we have seen that the armament cannot be of the heaviest; it may more often than not be individually less powerful than that of its opponent. The independent air fleet must therefore base its strength on its numerical superiority. It is precisely here that the need for homogeneity becomes manifest. Properly to assert the power of numbers, the whole fleet must come into action as nearly as possible as a single unit; in brief, it must concentrate the whole power of its combined fire on the numerically inferior enemy, and so take full advantage of the *n-square* law. No fleet can accomplish this unless its components are able to move and act in concert; thus the slowest vessel in a fleet must regulate its speed, and that which has the weakest armament the battle range.* In the case of the air fleet also we have the slowest climber determining the rate of ascent.

§ 95. *Air Tactics. Formation Flying.* In order that the air fleet shall be brought into action as a single unit, it is not only necessary that it should be in its constitution homogeneous, as already pointed out, but it must also be handled in some definite formation. Where the numbers are moderate, as, for example, in the handling of a single squadron, the formation adopted

* The range of the armament in an aerial engagement is mainly a question of muzzle velocity, not calibre.

AIR TACTICS. FORMATION FLYING. § 95

may evidently be fairly elastic, and there will be no difficulty in bringing the tail of the formation promptly into action. When, however, as we may suppose will some day be the case, the numbers become great the whole question cannot fail to become one of the first magnitude. The actual importance will again be greatly increased when air fleet meets air fleet, for in view of this eventuality, numbers will be augmented to an extent that we have as yet no means of gauging, perhaps beyond anything that we can at present imagine.

It would not serve any useful purpose in the present state of knowledge and development to attempt to discuss too closely the types of formation that may or may not be found suitable. We have the same, or an analogous, tactical problem in each of the older arms of the military organisation, and in the Navy, and in every case, in spite of the store of practical experience available, there is still a deal of controversy, different ideas being represented by different "schools" of thought; even in the case of the oldest Arm of the Service—the infantry, there is no unanimity of opinion. This being so, it would clearly be futile to attempt to lay down any scheme for an arm which cannot yet be said to exist. However, in spite of all this, there are certain outstanding facts that cannot fail to have some bearing, and will assuredly act as controlling influences.

§ 96. *Formation Flying. Airmanship and Signalling.* When the numbers become great a point will inevitably be reached when the accuracy and closeness of the formation will be a matter of first importance to the tactical scheme, since the only way in which the whole force can be brought to bear at once will be by a studied plan, in which each machine will have its allotted place. In other words, the number of machines from the point of view of the *n-square* law will no longer be the number

§ 96   AIRCRAFT IN WARFARE.

brought into the field by the strategic plan, but rather such portion of it as can be brought to bear simultaneously on the enemy; it will become a battle of airmanship. One of the difficulties which exists to-day, and probably will always be a matter of anxiety, is that of signalling; and to whatever extent this remains a difficulty, the flexibility of the formation will be impaired. The air fleet with the most perfect system of signalling will be the best able to take advantage of any opportunity that may arise in the course of an engagement by adapting its tactical scheme to the needs of the moment. In order to render it possible to control large numbers, it would appear to be evident that the unit command will be a small group, or what is at present termed a "flight" (some four or five strong), and that the individual machines will act on the plan of follow-my-leader; in other words, they will have instructions to keep station. It may be found desirable to extend the same system to larger units, as tending to avoid possible confusion.

§ 97. *The " V " formation and its value.* There is a point in connection with the pattern or character of these unit formations which may turn out to be of importance. It has for long been observed that certain birds, flying numbers strong (as in migration), are in the habit of assuming definite formation, and that this formation is of the shape of a letter V travelling point first; each bird, besides being some distance behind its leader, is also somewhat on one or the other flank. The reason for this is almost certainly one of aerodynamics; the air immediately in the wake of a bird in flight has residuary downward motion, and so is "bad" air from the point of view of the bird following. On the other hand, the air to the right and left of the leader has residuary upward motion owing to the vortical character of the wake disturbance, and so is "good" air; con-

AIR TACTICS. THE "V" FORMATION.   § 97

sequently the V formation arises naturally from each bird seeking the air which gives the best support, a matter in which most birds show consummate skill. There is very little doubt but that, by this manner of flight (formation flying in fact) a flight of birds is able to cover the ground with a material saving of work done. If the point in question is as important as it appears, it will certainly have to be taken into consideration in connection with aeroplane tactics, and more particularly formation flying. The follow-my-leader formation will evidently be on a V or diagonal plan rather than in line ahead.

§ 98. *Formation Flying. Machines disabled.* Whatever formation plan be adopted, it is evident that provision must be made for machines shot down or disabled to be able to leave the lines without creating confusion; evidently the closer the formation the more danger there will be of a real mix up and *débacle* in case of any confusion arising. Similarly, it is important that the enemy shall not be able, by ramming tactics or otherwise, to throw the formation out of gear; once more the "upper berth" clearly has every advantage.

§ 99. *Conditions in Aerial and Naval Tactics Contrasted.* The conditions, both as to armament and otherwise, which obtain in the Navy and in the Air Fleet offer many striking contrasts, the disparity is such as should preclude too much reliance being placed on analogies between the Services, except where the issue under consideration is of the broadest description.

The range of the gun-fire of an aeroplane (or other aircraft) is less a matter of the ultimate range of the gun employed than it is of the angular magnitude of the objective and of those other factors, such as speed and light, which contribute to render accurate shooting more or less difficult. In this the conditions differ remarkably from those which obtain in the Navy, where the useful

§ 99   AIRCRAFT IN WARFARE.

range is, roughly speaking, the ultimate effective range of the weapon employed. Thus in air warfare the craft carrying the heavier guns will in nowise possess the advantage that accrues in the corresponding case in the Navy. To a certain degree the larger aeroplane (or airship) will be penalised by the fact that it offers a target of greater area, and hence it will be more vulnerable. It may therefore be anticipated that the trend of design in the fighting machine will not be in the direction of very heavy units analogous to the battleship, but rather in the construction of machines of moderate size and weight, with the maximum possible rate of fire. As pointed out in one of the earlier articles, this *rate of fire* will be measured by the *number* of projectiles per second, rather than by their weight or striking energy. Whilst pointing out that the large aeroplane does not possess the marked advantage over the smaller, which, in the Navy, has led to the development of the Dreadnought and the super-Dreadnought, the author does not wish it to be inferred that his opinion is against the reasonable development and growth in the weight and dimensions of the fighting-machine. It may, indeed, be found when the size of air fleet becomes great, that, owing to the numbers becoming unwieldy, the only way in which the fighting strength can be increased will be by increasing the power of the individual unit—*i.e.*, by employing larger machines, mounting more guns.

Again, the larger machine, owing to its less relative body resistance and other well-understood causes, has a lower coefficient of traction, and so, where the speed is important (as we may always assume to be more or less the case), the advantage is with the larger machine. Alternatively, the larger machine, speed for speed, will, with equally good design, be the better climber; these points have already been discussed to some extent; it is

AIRCRAFT BASE AT HIGH ALTITUDE. § 99

only necessary here to draw attention to their influence. It would thus appear that there is nothing to be gained at the present time by attempting anything heroic in the direction of aeroplane design; the large machine will come (if it does come) by a natural process of evolution.

In contrast to the large machine the present author has frequently expressed the opinion that the single-man machine for many purposes would be able to effect all that is required of it (chiefly reconnaissance), and in this he has found himself opposed by the official specifications of the Departments concerned. However, the experience of the present war seems to indicate that there is something in this view, and it is more than probable that in the future the single-man machine will become a recognised type for military purposes. The advantage of the single-man type is that the machine can be altogether smaller and more compact, it can be designed to possess, speed for speed, a higher degree of inherent stability, and so will *fly itself*, leaving the pilot quite free to make observations and notes. Beyond this it is more difficult to hit and may more easily escape observation; it is also better to manage when it comes to alighting in a difficult situation. Needless to say, the single-man type is not a fighting type, although for bomb-dropping and such like duties it seems clear that the weight of a second man in extra bombs would be of far more value than the man himself.

§ 100. *Aircraft bases at High Altitude.* Aeronautical tactics will present many fascinating problems and opportunities to the air-fleet commander of the future, entirely without parallel in the pre-existing Arms of the Service, and there will be ample scope for originality and resource. Take, for example, the operations of aircraft in a mountainous country such as the Alpine regions of Europe; the selection of aeroplane stations;or

§ 100   AIRCRAFT IN WARFARE.

bases at high altitude, and their employment to determine an ascendancy over an enemy less fortunately situated; the utilisation to their full extent of air-currents, etc. It must be remembered that an advantage in altitude can be always turned to account to give a temporary advantage in speed, as in the swoop of a bird of prey. We may look confidently to the wide employment of such swooping tactics in the future of aerial warfare. The advantage possessed by an air fleet having its base at high altitude, sometimes even some 6,000 ft. or 8,000 ft. above sea-level, will be very great; it will have the initial advantage of the upper berth, and this under some circumstances may result in the enemy fleet, or sections of it, being kept flying for long periods together at high altitude in order to avoid the possibility of being engaged in action at a disadvantage. Such a process might conceivably result in the wearing away of a hostile air fleet to such a degree as to determine its ultimate defeat.

CHAPTER XV.
(December 11th, 1914).

THE COMMAND OF THE AIR AND ITS LIMITATIONS. INTERNATIONAL QUESTIONS RELATING TO AIRCRAFT IN WAR.

§ 101. *The Command of the Air, and its Limitations.* The term "command of the air" can never be taken to carry a meaning so wide or far-reaching, or in any sense so comprehensive, as that understood when we speak of the "command of the sea." Sea-power has its origin and secret in the fact that (as rightly insisted by Mahan) the seas control the main highways of international commerce and communication; thus sea-power is necessarily world-power. It would not, strictly speaking, be true to say that the command of the sea essentially involves world-wide supremacy; but so far as a navy is provided with fully equipped bases, so far will its power extend in its plenitude. It has sometimes been rashly assumed by writers that in the future air-power is not only going to exercise an influence as wide-spread and decisive as sea-power, but is, in fact, about to take a superior position, and that the latter will lose some of its present character and importance. No such conclusion can at present be justified. It is, of course, to-day considered bad form to call any engineering project *impossible;* but in view of the fact that, after making every reasonable allowance for possible developments, the maximum distance that can be flown by an aeroplane without replenishment is less than 2,000 miles, it is clear that the range or radius of action of an air fleet must be regarded as permanently imposing strict limitations on its employment. The large airship, even should it be found to be of greater military or naval importance than suggested in the present volume, is scarcely likely to be better situated, and suffers from the not inconsiderable disadvantage of requiring accommodation of an elaborate and expensive kind. Hence we see that the "command of the air" is, from a world standpoint, a local condition. It might conceivably be secured and asserted by a European Power over half the continent of Europe, or the whole of the south and east of the African continent might be dominated by air fleets having their bases in Egypt and other territory in British occupation. Even this, however, is looking a great way ahead. For the time being we may take it that the policy of any one of the Great Powers in time of peace will be to secure unquestioned supremacy within its own territorial limits, with such bases in the vicinity of its coast lines and frontiers as will suffice to ensure the respect of hostile aircraft in the event of an outbreak of war. When a state of war exists, the task of an air fleet will be to maintain its air supremacy at home, and to extend and carry the command of the air over land or water in support of the Army and Navy, wherever operating. Hence the Aeronautical Force is not to be considered as a new kind of Navy, or otherwise as a self-contained Service to which large-scale independent duties can be assigned; it is definitely, in the words of our title, a new or Fourth *Arm*.

§ 102. *Neutral Aircraft. International Regulations*. It has been believed from the earliest days of the modern aeronautical movement that the military (and naval) uses of the flying-machine would prove to be one of the most important of its initial applications. This view has been more than justified, so much so

INTERNATIONAL REGULATIONS. § 102

that to-day there is scarcely a machine that "takes the air" in Europe which is not on Service duty. This fact probably the most ardent supporter of the military usage of the flying-machine would have scarcely ventured to predict prior to the outbreak of hostilities. Certainly, if five or six years ago anyone had been bold enough to assert that at the beginning of the year 1915 there would be scarcely a machine flying in Europe on other than military duty, it would have sounded incredible. That the present situation is not representative of the future in this respect we may take for granted. On the other hand, it is becoming clear that we may quite dismiss from our minds any general usage of the air as a commercial highway; the traffic in merchandise which will be air-borne will never become a great percentage of the world's total.

We may anticipate that lines will be established for the rapid conveyance of mails, and to some extent we may look to the development of passenger services in different parts of the world. But for the time being the inconvenient (and, in the case of shipping, contentious) question as to the rights of neutrals in the air can scarcely be said to have been established; commercial usage of the air is virtually non-existent.

The obligations imposed by international law and convention on both belligerents and neutrals are, at the best, of an arbitrary and makeshift character; it is doubtful whether anything is to be gained by attempting to lay down a code or set of rules to control a form of locomotion, in its application to warfare, when so little experience is available. However, the author has had a book placed in his hands (published early in 1914) on "Aircraft in War," in which the whole contents, from cover to cover, relate to nothing but the international aspect of the subject and to rival codes of proposed

§ 102 AIRCRAFT IN WARFARE.

"legislation." It seems, therefore, that this side of the subject requires discussion. Without wishing to belittle work of the type in question, it may certainly be said that the discussion of anything more than the barest generalities of the subject can only be time and effort wasted. A new Arm requires to work out its own salvation in warfare, and the machine which has won for itself and mankind the freedom of the air is not to have its future proscribed or fettered by the scratchings of an unofficial quill.

§ 103. *Belligerent Aircraft and the Rights and Obligations of Neutrals.* A question which appears likely to lead to great trouble in practice is the propriety of belligerent aircraft operating over the territory of a neutral Power. Without discussing such academic subjects as the territorial sovereignty of the air, it seems clear that eventually neither belligerent can be prevented from passing over neutral territory except by the air forces and counter-air forces of the neutral Power in question. If such Power should elect not to use his forces to prevent such violation of his territorial air, it will be impossible in practice to make him do so or hold him responsible. Beyond this, if the neutral Power should subsequently make claim against a belligerent for using his air, it is difficult to see how any such claim could have more ground than an ordinary civil claim for trespass, in which the only admissible basis of an award is for damage done. If the aircraft has flown at reasonable altitude and has done no injury by dropping anything, or by gun-fire, it is difficult to see how any claim could be substantiated. If the neutral Power should elect to employ his aircraft and counter aircraft artillery to assert a presumed right to his territorial air, he not only puts himself to very considerable expense and inconvenience, but at the best

RIGHTS AND OBLIGATIONS OF NEUTRALS. § 103

his efforts are unlikely to be wholly effective; in thick weather the whole of a belligerent air fleet might pass over his territory without once being sighted. Hence it will be possible that at any time he may be plausibly accused of favouring one side or the other, and thus find himself in difficulties of a diplomatic kind far worse than would have been possible had he left his air undefended. A host of other difficulties spring into one's mind in connection with the defence of territorial air by a neutral Power; aircraft may encounter above the clouds: a belligerent fleet and the neutral air-sentry force. How shall they decide in what way to act? They cannot stand still and hold a palaver whilst the matter is tested by a plumb-line. Clearly any attempt to enforce neutrality in territorial air would be more likely to drag the neutral Power into the war on one side or the other than a rigid abstinence from interference; and since this is one of the most important contingencies to be guarded against,* it seems evident that, *as a matter of expediency*, the rights (if they be admitted) of neutrals over their territorial air should be regarded as not involving any obligation of action against belligerent aircraft. On the other hand, it is equally clear that the ordinary powers of enforcing restrictions in such matters as flying over prohibited areas, etc., will in nowise be weakened by the existence of a state of war, and neither belligerent will have cause for complaint if his aircraft, after due warning, should be fired upon. In brief, whilst it would appear to be impossible to deny the right to a neutral of chasing away—or, if necessary, even of destroying—belligerent aircraft if found in occupation of territorial air, it would appear to be equally impossible to impose the duty of doing so as an obligation. A

* It is, in fact, one of the main benefits of an international code that the friction between neutrals and belligerents should be minimised.

§ 103 AIRCRAFT IN WARFARE.

corollary to this would appear to be that the use of a neutral's territorial air will only become a violation of neutrality if persisted in in the presence of aircraft or air forces of the neutral Power.* Put in a few words, the position, as above, is in every way analogous to the ordinary law of trespass; the owner is entitled to turn the trespasser off, using only such force as is necessary, and can claim damages only on account of actual injury sustained.

§ 104. *Other International Questions Relating to Aircraft. Distinctive Marks.* It has been suggested, or stated, by most previous writers on the subject that aircraft will be *required* to carry a distinctive mark or colours, indicating their nationality and their character as military or belligerent—*i.e.*, not civilian—machines. This view is clearly based on the practice which is presumed to obtain in the case of ships-of-war, and which is, to some extent, necessary owing to the fact that the ocean being the common highway of all maritime nations, some declaration of nationality is obligatory, or at least desirable, from the point of view of neutrals as well as of belligerents. History has shown again and again that when a state of war exists, no rules, codified or otherwise, will compel a war-vessel or fleet to display its national flag, or prevent it from using the flag of any other nation that may commend itself at the moment; and if it were not for the interest of neutrals, the practice of employing any distinguishing flag or mark in war-time might fall into desuetude without affecting anything or anybody. Now, in the case of aircraft, it is not only improbable, but quite inconceivable, that civilians or neutrals will be permitted to fly at all in or near the zone

---

* If this view be accepted, the recent action of the British naval airmen in passing over Swiss territory is quite permissible and in no way irregular. Switzerland, had she so willed, could have employed aircraft to police her frontiers, in order to prevent the "borrowing" of her territorial air. Failing this, and not having suffered actual, i e., material, injury, she has no ground of complaint.

NATIONAL OR DISTINCTIVE MARKS.   § 104

of hostilities. It is even probable that on the declaration of war all private aircraft will be requisitioned or impounded (as now done in the case of wireless telegraphic apparatus), and that neutrals will be advised that they will use the territorial air of the belligerent countries entirely at their own risk and peril; in fact, that they will be shot down if detected. We cannot for an instant admit a state of things such as would arise were neutral or private aircraft (with war correspondents and suchlike) allowed to fly in any area in which fighting might be in progress; there would be continual uncertainty as to the nationality of such alien aircraft, and no means of checking the abuse of a neutral flag by spies or imposters. The position is totally different from that which obtains at sea. There is no possible means of investigation, and no time to ask questions; if there is any doubt, instant action is imperative. It is only too evident that even if distinguishing marks were agreed, no reliance would be placed upon their genuineness in real warfare, and their disuse, sooner or later, may be considered to be a foregone conclusion.

It will be part of the business of the airmen and gunners of both belligerent armies to be fully conversant with the peculiarities of the various types of aircraft in their own service and in that of the enemy, and to be sufficiently "fly" to detect any attempts at disguise or deception. It is, of course, always open to the aircraft of either army to carry a distinguishing mark or sign which can be displayed at will, and the nature of this may either be known or unknown to the enemy; it may, to ensure secrecy, be changed from time to time like a "pass-word." This, however, is an entirely different matter to the compulsory wearing of a badge, like a uniform or a national flag, by which the nationality will be openly declared as a matter of obligation.

§ 105   AIRCRAFT IN WARFARE.

§ 105. *Aircraft landing in Neutral Territory.* Other questions of an international character relating to aircraft do not appear to present any serious difficulty. Evidently a belligerent aircraft descending into neutral territory will be interned, just as would a cavalryman or an armoured motor-car. To treat an aeroplane or airship according to the rule established in the case of a warship would clearly be to admit its right to have been in the territorial air of the neutral Power concerned, which, we may assume, will be considered quite inadmissible. Already, in the course of the present war, we have seen the hospitality of neutrals greatly abused. It certainly is not just or expedient that the cruisers of a nation which has ceased to possess any coaling stations, or bases, of its own should be allowed to roam indefinitely at large, interfering with the commerce of an enemy, when such action would have been impossible without neutral assistance. The proof of the inexpediency of the existing rule in such a case is to be found in the fact that the difficulty could be soon ended by a few declarations of war against some of the minor neutral Powers, with the bombardment of the ports by which the enemy is served. The very fact that this becomes the logical reply, which, but for humanitarian considerations, would without doubt be pursued, demonstrates an inherent deficiency in the present international code, and one which perhaps may, in due course, be remedied. Any rule by which aircraft would be enabled to utilise neutral territory or neutral resources for repair, refit, or replenishment would almost certainly be the cause of great friction, and might result in a position so impossible as to drag the neutral Power into the conflict, the precise eventuality that it should be an object of international convention to avoid.*

In other respects there would seem to be no reason

* Footnote page following.

LANDING IN NEUTRAL TERRITORY. § 105

to treat the flying-machine or dirigible differently from arms or armament of other kinds, or belligerent airmen differently from other combatants. It is at least clear that any modifications in the accepted code which may eventually be found necessary may well be left to come as the natural outgrowth from experience in warfare. With regard to the manufacture and supply of aircraft by neutrals to belligerents, or the granting of facilities of transport, the same considerations will govern the decision of the neutral Power as are at present involved where arms and munitions of other kinds are concerned. The Power affected requires to consider in what way its own interests and those of neutrality are best served.

---

* It would often appear from the framing of clauses and debates in connection with the various international conferences that the above (in the author's opinion the most important object of achievement of international conventions) is almost lost sight of in a quagmire of dangerous and namby-pamby sentimentality. In many cases the desire seems to be vaguely to *do something that will be thought humane*; no clear idea seems to exist as to right and proper grounds on which regulations of restrictions should be based. Thus, for example, in the Brussels Conference of 1874, Article 13 *e*, and in the Hague Conference of 1899, Article 23 *e* (already cited, Chapter VII.), the same restriction appears for the prohibition of bullets of the dum-dum or expanding type; in the first (the abortive Conference of 1874) the prohibition is worded.—" The use of arms, projectiles, or material *of a nature to cause unnecessary suffering*, the wording adopted at the later conference is " . . . *of a nature to cause superfluous injury.*" At the 1874 Conference the assembly was, it appears, imbued with feelings of horror for pain and suffering, but in 1899 this seems to have become changed for a dread of disablement and death—a totally different matter The suggested prohibition of bombs or missiles from aircraft is an illustration of the same infirmity of purpose that appears to reign supreme at peace conferences and the like; again we see the dictates of fear mistaken for those of benevolence. There is, and was, no evidence that bombs from aeroplanes or balloons are any more barbarous or inhumanly destructive than the shells from artillery or howitzer batteries, yet clauses were debated and framed, and (with a time-limit restriction) were actually signed by certain of the representatives of the Powers. The *fear of the unknown* is without doubt more widespread and potent than its victims realise. A cavalryman is killed in peace time by a fall from his horse, it scarcely excites comment, an army airman falls and is killed and a thrill of horror goes through the country—it is *a new kind o death*.

CHAPTER XVI.
(December 24th, 1914).

PRESENT DAY POSITION AND FUTURE OF THE FOURTH ARM.

§ 106. *The Fourth Arm in Peace Time.* The problems connected with the maintenance of the Fourth Arm in time of peace are numerous, and present difficulties which will certainly be found to increase as the numerical strength of the Arm is augmented. It is not easy to form any real conception of what the future may have in store in the direction of numbers, but as a matter of guesswork it is difficult to believe that, sooner or later, the strength of the Flying Corps will not reach or exceed 1 per cent. of the number of bayonets. Thus a considerable part of the work formerly allotted to cavalry will in the future be assigned to the new Arm, and the cavalry ordinarily represents from 5 to 10 per cent. of the number of bayonets. Also, the guns will require the assistance of aircraft, probably one or more machines being attached to each battery or group. Beyond this there will be specialised fighting-machines of different denominations. Taking everything into consideration, the suggested 1 per cent. does not look like an overestimate; it is probably too low.

Assuming 1 per cent. as a basis, the numbers are already formidable. Thus, for the British regulars on home service prior to the outbreak of war, the number would need to be at least some 1,000 machines. In the case of the large Continental armies—say, the French—with over 700,000 men (peace footing), it may be

THE FOURTH ARM IN PEACE TIME. § 106

anticipated that a total of about 5,000 machines will be required.[*]

The peace training of these vast numbers of flying-men would represent an organisation of immense proportions, especially if the author's anticipations in such matters as aeronautical tactics, formation flying, etc., come to be realised. The multiplicity of flight-grounds, training-schools, workshops, sheds, etc., with the necessary staff of instructors, mechanics, and other non-combatant members of the organisation, will render the whole matter a very big undertaking.

In view of the probable magnitude of the business, it is to be feared that the question of peace-time casualties in the Flying Corps will inevitably become a matter of the most serious importance. It is quite certain that everything possible must be done to minimise the dangers of military flying in peace time; this looks like a self-evident proposition, but apparently it is not. The author has frequently passed comment on the seriously defective nature of some of the existing flight-grounds, and has found himself met (quite unofficially) by the argument that since the men will have to alight upon pasture land, or even ploughed fields, when on service, it is best that they should have plenty of experience of rough ground when at home; further, that it is necessary to test the strength of the machines by using them in peace time under service conditions. So far as the machine is concerned, this kind of argument is altogether unsound. If the *type* is one which has been thoroughly tested in the first instance before adoption, and if the machines are properly inspected during manufacture, they will be far more reliable in the battlefield if they have not been knocked about by rough treatment over

[*] The fact should not be lost sight of that Great Britain may require to regulate the strength of her Flying Corps by that of her neighbours rather than by the strength of her own Army

§ 106   AIRCRAFT IN WARFARE.

bad ground in peace-time flying. Testing to destruction is good in its way, but the particular article so tested must not be subsequently used. With regard to the men themselves, the argument that a bad ground is better than a good one is almost as gravely at fault. One hundred alightings on a good ground (with a fair surface and without obstructions) will carry less risk than, say, 20 or 30 on a poor or bad ground, and the man who has made his 100 alightings, with, if we wish, *imaginary* obstacles, is a better man than the one who has only done his 20 or 30, especially if the latter is disabled or dead. A man who practises jumping uses a light lath, which will do him no injury if he falls, in spite of the fact that his object may be to join a club of harriers and jump a five-bar gate.

The need for improvement in our flying grounds is very much emphasised, when the importance of night flying is taken into consideration. With bad or indifferent flight grounds, such as existent at the time of the outbreak of war, alighting by night is an operation of extreme risk, and is only possible for a pilot of great experience. There is no real reason why alighting by night should be unduly dangerous; flight grounds of adequate area, properly drained, and of good surface, are however essential. There are many ways, by means of artificial lights, by which the difficulty of judging the distance from the ground may be overcome.

It is more than possible that, in some respects and from certain points of view, flying by night may become less hazardous than by daylight, just as, for example, there are many conditions under which navigation at sea is actually safer by night than by day.

The military importance of night flying is in part due to the need for countering the activity of the larger dirigible or Zeppelin, but the question is far wider than

NIGHT PLYING. ALIGHTING GROUNDS. § 106

this. At present all raids, reconnaissances and other duties entrusted to the aeroplane are subject to the condition that the operation must be completed in time to return to headquarters before dark; infraction of this condition is prone to result in serious losses, both of machines and men. It is abundantly clear that no such restriction should be tolerated, and the solution of the difficulty is to be sought in the provision of flight grounds, worthy of our present day aircraft. It is a serious reflection on our conduct as a nation that we have so far shown ourselves prepared to spend more money in the provision and upkeep of cricket fields, than we are ready to do for the safety of our flying men and the efficiency of the Aeronautical Arm.

Even before the outbreak of the present war, the author had more than once given expression to the opinion that our flight grounds stood more in need of immediate improvement than the machines themselves. Thus the following is quoted from the author's recent " James Forest " lecture (1914) :—

"There is, moreover, another factor (quite extraneous to flying conditions proper) that at present puts a definite handicap on high speed and prevents the aeronautical designer from doing himself justice in that direction; namely, the backward condition of existing accommodation in the way of alighting-grounds. Owing to quite well-understood conditions, it is necessary, before rising, to attain a speed on the ground not very much less than the normal flight-speed of the machine, and so, in the case of a machine designed for 120 miles per hour maximum flight-velocity, it would be necessary to acquire a speed round about 80 miles per hour before leaving the ground, which would necessitate a straight-line run of about 300 yards. To comply with this condition, and to give safe room otherwise for handling the machine, a flight-ground of at least half-mile length should be provided, having a surface far better than is now customary. Beyond this, since in bad weather it is undesirable

§ 106 AIRCRAFT IN WARFARE.

either to start or to alight across the direction of the wind, it would appear that a ground of not less than some 100 or 150 acres in extent would be desirable. At the present time the Author believes that the provision of well-appointed flight-grounds of the area stated in different parts of the country would do more to further the cause of aviation than an equal expenditure of money in any other direction.

"It is possible that at some future time the landing-gear of machines may be so far improved that it may be found possible to alight on the ordinary high road; also it may be that sections of the high road will be specially widened and freed from adjacent obstruction to serve in cases of emergency. It is clear, however, that the general use of the high road for this purpose would in any case be open to very grave objection.

"It might be thought that the setting apart as flight-grounds of such considerable areas of land as above indicated would impose too serious a financial burden on flying, at least for some time to come, to be commercially possible. It is, however, to be borne in mind that with proper management such grounds could, especially if duplicated, be utilized for grazing purposes: thus, if an area of 200 acres were available, a herd of some few hundred head of cattle could be grazed, being transferred from one section of the ground to another from time to time. It is therefore evident that, under favourable conditions, the commercial aspect of the problem is by no means outrageous, even during the period that must intervene before flying as a mode of locomotion can become in any sense popular. Beyond this, assuming that the flying-machine is able to justify its existence apart from its employment by the Services, there seems no reason to suppose that the returns of a well-equipped flying-ground might not easily become far greater than the agricultural value of the land concerned, which at the best is but a few pounds per annum per acre."

§ 107. *The Fourth Arm in Peace Time. Depreciation and Obsolescence.* A somewhat knotty point is that of the duration of the service life of aircraft. So far no definition has been generally accepted. The

PLATE XII.

AN EXAMPLE OF ROUGH USAGE. The Sopwith "Scout," a very fast Single Seater. After an upset due to bad landing. The wing structure bore the shock and weight; the Pilot escaped injury.

DEPRECIATION AND OBSOLESCENCE.   § 107

truth is that any machine may become "superannuated" either owing to *depreciation* or to *obsolescence*; in the former case the number of miles covered will be the determining factor, coupled, perhaps, with other facts relating to its history or usage; in the latter, it is the age of the machine which determines its unfitness for service, considered, of course, in relation to the advance which has been made in the art of construction since the date of building. Thus a machine may be unfit for service either because it is, according to some accepted definition, *worn out* and incapable of repair, or because it is *obsolete in design*. In some cases obsolescence may be absolute, as when a design is so out of date that by comparison with the best available it is to be considered unsafe or uneconomical; in this case it is only fit to be destroyed; or its obsolescence may be relative, as when it is outclassed by the machines of corresponding type in the service of some neighbouring Power; in this case it is fit to be sold out of the Service or to be transferred to some distant part of the Empire, where competition is not equally severe. The questions of depreciation and obsolescence and the disposal of condemned machines have not yet received due consideration. On continuous active service it would appear that the life of a present day aeroplane is about three or four months.

The foregoing may be taken merely as samples of the many questions which have to be faced before the training of army pilots and aeroplane gunners and signallers can be attempted in the thousands, or tens of thousands, for which the warfare of the future may call. Without adequate consideration of these questions, coupled with appropriate measures, progress in the direction of increase of numbers and the practical development of aeroplane tactics on a large scale will be most seriously handicapped.

§ 108   AIRCRAFT IN WARFARE.

§ 108. *Present Position. British Superiority.* The reports as to the performance of the air-craft, and more particularly the aeroplanes, of the different belligerent armies are at present very meagre and incomplete. However, it would appear from the observations of those best qualified to judge that the British machines are by no means backward, and in many important respects are superior both to those of the enemy and to those of our Allies. The features in which we at present possess the advantage are those in which the flying capacity of the machine, rather than its more essentially fighting quality, is concerned. Thus superiority may be claimed for the British aeroplanes: firstly, as being better aerodynamically—that is to say, for given horse-power and weight they possess a greater speed and climbing power; secondly, they are more stable—in fact, our present-day machines are definitely automatically or inherently stable; thirdly, they have a higher factor of safety than any of their Continental rivals and are far more robust as to alighting gear; and, fourthly, they are more weather-proof. In short, they are better fitted to service conditions. Beyond this, one of the latest models turned out by the Royal Aircraft Factory is by far the fastest machine in the world, being some ten or twenty miles per hour faster than anything the Continent can show. On the other hand, on the outbreak of hostilities we found ourselves without a thoroughly satisfactory fighting or gun-carrying type of machine—it is one matter to be able to mount a gun on an aeroplane, and quite another to design and construct machines expressly for that purpose. It is, indeed, doubtful whether at that date any really satisfactory gun-carrying aeroplane existed at all; it is in any case precisely in this direction that our own air service has found itself most lacking. In brief, it may fairly and undoubtedly

PLATE XIII.

R.A.F. TYPE S.E.4. Single Seat Reconnaissance Machine.
Maximum Speed over 130 Miles per hour.

ASCENDENCY OF BRITISH AIRCRAFT. § 108

be claimed that so far as the reconnaissance machine is concerned, the British aircraft are more than able to hold their own with those of the other European nations. In the main the "proprietary" machines built by private firms have lacked the all-round qualities of those turned out by the Government factory, or under contract to the Royal Aircraft Factory specification. In some cases they have failed from a constructional standpoint; under the exacting conditions of service the alighting chassis have sometimes proved inadequate; in other cases the weather-proof qualities of the "proprietary" machines have been found deficient. These defects have not only shown themselves amongst British-built machines, but also some of the best known of the French makes have failed, or at least are reported to have cut a very sorry figure when submitted to the rigorous test of service conditions in real warfare. Possibly it was not anticipated (as it appears is the case) that machines would be required to remain permanently in the open night and day, shelter being the exception rather than the rule. It is under these conditions that our own Aircraft Factory machines have exhibited an unrivalled robustness of constitution. On behalf of the "proprietary" makes of machine, however, it must be said that some of the most notable of the exploits performed by the Naval Air Service (such as the raids on Düsseldorf and Friedrichshafen) have been performed by such machines,[*] which proves that, from the point of view of

[*] The execution of these sensational feats of arms by our naval airmen must not be taken to mean that they could not have been performed equally well by members of the Royal Flying Corps, but rather that the latter are fully occupied by their regular daily work of military reconnaissance, and are certainly no more than numerically sufficient for the needs of our Army in the field. In the Navy, the routine or "business" employment of aircraft (more especially aeroplanes) is not yet understood; the efficient patrolling by aircraft of the seas in which a state of war exists—mainly the North Sea, in the present instance—should be considered by the Air Department of the Admiralty to be its most important duty; this will require the systematic employment of a considerable fleet of aeroplanes, which should, if possible, be machines of 16 or 18 hours' capacity and at least capable of 80 miles per hour. The large airship, until recently in contemplation for this duty, provides, in the author's opinion, a doubtful solution, without recapitulation of its other

§ 108   AIRCRAFT IN WARFARE.

flying, they are fully worthy of the Service and a credit to their designers and constructors.

§ 109. *Causes which have Contributed to British Ascendancy.* The position of the British in the matter of military aeronautics—more particularly aviation—to-day, which, subject to the limitations stated, may properly be described as "ascendancy," is not to be attributed to any one definite cause; the results achieved in the field have been contributed to both by the personnel of our Flying Corps and Naval Air Service, and by the sound qualities of the machines employed. In view of the peace-time exploits of the airmen of the three leading Western Powers, in which it may fairly be said that honours have been divided, it would appear that, without belittling the magnificent performance and daring of our flying men, it is in the matter of material—*i.e.*, actual machines, etc.—that our superiority is most marked.*

In discussing the influences which have led to the development of the present-day types of service machine it must be borne in mind that these influences have been at work in the factories of the private firms engaged equally with the Government factory at Farnborough. There has in the past been little or no secrecy in connection with the Royal Aircraft Factory—private builders and the designers attached to private firms have virtually had the "run of the place," and all possible assistance has been rendered them; in brief, the private firm has been at all times kept thoroughly up-to-date in the matter of technical information.

deficiencies, it is *too slow*; the key-note in matters of military or naval advancement is *mobility*, the measure of which is flight speed. As in certain other fields of employment, the dirigible might prove better suited to the work in question than the aeroplane, were it not for the fact that sooner or later, the aircraft of the enemy will have to be faced. The inherent weakness of the slow and vulnerable balloon type cannot fail to place it at a disadvantage.

* In time of peace the opportunities for public demonstration accorded to Service machines are limited Since the time of writing it has become apparent that our superiority is no less due to our men and organisation than to the merits of our machines

WORK OF THE ADVISORY COMMITTEE. § 109

The main factors that have contributed to the production of the machines of outstanding merit, which are upholding our reputation in the field to-day, are unquestionably the greater scientific knowledge possessed by our designers, and the conspicuous ability shown by the staff of the Royal Aircraft Factory in making practical use and application of the latest and best information at their disposal, and in their own full-scale experimental work and study of the many practical problems outside the range of purely scientific research.

The machinery set up by the Government for dealing with a new and difficult question of the greatest national importance, has, so far as its allotted scope is concerned, worked with singular smoothness and undeniable effect. In brief, we have the Royal Aircraft Factory, which may be regarded as the headquarters of the national sources of production, and in itself of the character of an experimental or pioneer department rather than a national manufactory. Behind this we have the Advisory Committee for Aeronautics, a body whose functions are mainly concerned with scientific and technical questions, and at the disposal of the Advisory Committee a large and growing department forming part of the National Physical Laboratory. In addition to this, there exists the Naval side, consisting of constructional works and depôt at Aldershot, which has taken over in its entirety the Dirigible (Balloon) section of the work.

The secretarial headquarters of the Advisory Committee is permanently located at the National Physical Laboratory, the Director of the latter, Dr. R. T. Glazebrook, F.R.S., being the Chairman of the Committee under the presidency of Lord Rayleigh, O.M., F.R.S.; the Army being represented by the Director-General of Military Aeronautics, Major-General Sir David Henderson, K.C.B., the Navy by the Director of the

§ 109   AIRCRAFT IN WARFARE.

Air Department of the Admiralty, Captain Murray F. Sueter, and the Royal Aircraft Factory by the Superintendent, Mr. Mervyn O'Gorman, C.B. In a sense the Advisory Committee may be said to act as a "clearing-house" for information, inasmuch as its functions are to ensure, on the one hand, that the information obtained from the work done at the National Physical Laboratory, and collected from other sources, is duly made available to the Royal Aircraft Factory and to the Services, and, on the other hand, to hear and dispose of the difficulties and demands of the said parties. This latter may be a matter either of tendering immediate advice or of appropriately employing the resources of the National Physical Laboratory, or requisitioning *any* such other assistance as may be deemed expedient. The work is carried out in the main on an annual programme framed on a sufficiently elastic basis to allow of all possible contingencies being dealt with. In addition to the foregoing, the Committee receive and publish a considerable number of new investigations, also abstracts of most of the work of importance done on the Continent; in these latter respects the work accomplished by the Committee can be best judged from a perusal of the Annual Report presented to Parliament.[*] It is by these means that those responsible for the design, specification, and construction of our aircraft, whether military or naval, have been, and are, kept fully informed of all that concerns them from both technical and scientific standpoints, and have been able to employ the somewhat limited resources granted them by the Treasury to the best possible advantage. Beyond this the staff of the Royal Aircraft Factory includes men of exceptional resource and ability, who have proved themselves again and again more than competent in the execution of the duties entrusted to their care. It is

[*] Reports 1909-10, 1910-11, 1911-12, and 1912-13, at present published.

EARLY (EXPERIMENTAL) MODEL OF B.E.2c Calculated and Demonstrated as inherently stable by the late Mr. E. T. Busk. *Compare Plate III.*

VALUE OF SCIENTIFIC GROUNDWORK. § 109

impossible in this connection to pass over without mention the great loss which the factory (and the country, it may be said), has suffered in the death of Mr. E. T. Busk, who recently lost his life in the execution of his duties, being burnt to death in mid-air whilst personally carrying out investigations of an experimental character. Mr. Busk combined with exceptional ability as an experimenter a very thorough knowledge of his work; he was largely responsible for the design and construction of many instruments and appliances which have proved of the greatest service in the development of the present-day machine.

There are many of the less-informed members of the public who believe that the flying-machine has been developed, and is to-day being designed, by empirical methods, and that the scientific man has had nothing to do with it, except, perhaps, late in the day, to give plausible explanations of the "whys and wherefores." Nothing is further from the truth. The work relating to the design and construction of the modern aeroplane is quite as much the result of careful and scientific calculation, in fact, rather more so, than in the case of shipbuilding. All matters connected with the flying properties of a machine, whether it be lifting power, propulsion, or stability, are amenable to rigorous scientific treatment, and are as carefully founded on scale-model and wind-channel experiment as the analogous problems in ship design.

In scientific work connected with flight (as pointed out by the author in his recent James Forrest Lecture), the work which has been done in this country is far in advance of that done on the Continent; more especially is this the case in connection with stability: it is fair to take it that the advantageous position in which Britain finds herself to-day in the matter of aircraft is legitimately

§ 109 AIRCRAFT IN WARFARE.

to be regarded as a reflection of this fact. No one acquainted with the history of the development of our Service machines can have the slightest doubt as to the truth of this statement.

CHAPTER XVII.
(December 24th, 1914)

THE MAINTENANCE OF BRITISH SUPREMACY.
GOVERNMENT VERSUS PRIVATE MANUFACTURE.
CONTINUITY OF POLICY. SCHEME OF CONTROL.
A BOARD OF AERONAUTICAL CONSTRUCTION.

§ 110. *Maintenance of British Supremacy.* The maintenance of the present superiority of the British reconnaissance machine and the development of different types, and, in short, the building up and consolidation of the Aeronautical Arm, both as to quality and quantity, in order to ensure our capacity to hold our own with the other great Powers, is a task of national importance, and, as such, one of the first magnitude. In order that our Aeronautical Arm may be raised and maintained as a whole at the necessary high degree of efficiency, more will be needed than merely the technical superiority of our machines; many other questions of vital consequence will require to be adequately dealt with. However, the basis of strength lies in possessing the right types of machine in adequate numbers. Hence there must be no relaxation of effort; we must retain our technical ascendancy by every means in our power.

There is much to be said at the outset in favour of the exercise of greater secrecy in the matter of technical information. At present a great deal of work of an important character is done at the public expense which is of the utmost value to the aeronautical constructor, and forthwith it is given complete publicity; one has only to glance through any one of the annual reports of the Advisory Committee to realise the extent to which this

§ 110   AIRCRAFT IN WARFARE.

is the case. There is, it is true, also a certain amount of work which is not published, being considered as of a confidential character. The question arises whether the main body of the work, or, at least, some of the more important sections, should not be held back, and treated as confidential for a certain period, possibly one complete year, in order to give our own designers a twelve months' lead. The difficulties in the way of any such scheme are, firstly, that, to be effective, the first twelve months' output of any new design would require to be met as output from the Government factory; the conditions issued with designs and specifications for tenders, though nominally intended to ensure secrecy, can never be really effective. Secondly, in a branch of Governmental activity as little understood by the public as that of aeronautical construction, the public and Parliament expect to see something for their money, and for those entrusted with aeronautical development to have shrunk from publicity would have been equivalent to committing suicide. In spite of any disadvantage which may have resulted from publicity in the past, the net result has been highly satisfactory. It is more than probable, however, that the Continental Powers have somewhat underrated the importance of the work which had been done in this country, and have taken no particular pains to follow or study that work; this neglect is not likely to be repeated. Certain it is that, technically, the Continental nations are, without being aware of the fact, some way behind us in aeroplane design. The author is disposed to think that, all things considered, it will be found advisable in the future to restrict publication somewhat, and considerably to strengthen the Aircraft Factory, to enable full control to be exercised over new models, and otherwise to take steps to ensure secrecy where, in the national interest, it may be deemed wise.

THE QUESTION OF MANUFACTURE. § 111

§ 111. *Government versus Private Manufacture.* In every problem of production in quantity, otherwise that which is termed "manufacture," the essence of true economy is *continuity*. The whole of the organisation of a modern factory is based on the work in progress being of the nature of a "flow," rather than a succession of jerks. In actual practice it is only in the case of certain industries in which the goods manufactured are not liable to change from year to year, and in which the demand is not of a fluctuating character, that the "flow" can be maintained under ideal conditions—that is to say, with perfect uniformity. In other cases fluctuations are inevitable; changes in design necessitated by the stress of competition and the advance of knowledge prevent the condition of perfect continuity from being realised. Under these conditions a not inconsiderable part of the duties of the organisation is that concerned with negotiating the necessary irregularities and changes. The work still is dealt with on the theory that it remains a flow, but it is actually a succession of batches, the flow being comparable to that of a river subject to seasonal fluctuations, periods of flood alternating with periods of slack. The system of organisation requires to be framed to deal with the consequent unavoidable breakages of continuity, and it is the business of the works and engineering staff so to regulate the progress of work that the resulting disorganisation is minimised, and the economy of production is not too seriously impaired. The possibilities of the situation, so far as the management staff is concerned, are very much circumscribed by considerations of finance and the exigencies of the market. These latter questions are, or should be, dominated by the prevision of the directorate; they are matters governed by the *policy* of the company, for which the board of directors (directly or through their managing

§ 111   AIRCRAFT IN WARFARE.

director) should be definitely responsible. The *policy* thus includes such questions as the market or markets to be attacked; the quantities and dates at which it is estimated sales can be effected; the financial needs, whether it be for building or plant extensions or for stock-in-trade; and the provision of, or the raising of, the necessary finance.

In brief, in a well-managed concern the Board may be said to control that which is in military parlance the strategy of the company, whilst the management staff look after the tactics. Clearly, just as in military affairs, success must depend very largely upon the strategic scheme being accommodated to the tactical resources, and the tactical work being skilfully adapted to the strategic scheme.

Now, in the case of a Government factory, there is no real board of directors. The financial side is controlled by the Treasury, whose interests are not concerned with the prosperity of the concern in the least degree; it is equally satisfactory from a Treasury standpoint whether the "grant" can be reduced by the most arbitrary and expensive "cheeseparing," or whether it is done by legitimate and proper means—by the exercise of true economy. The result is that anyone acquainted with the working of Government manufacturing institutions could cite innumerable cases of gross extravagance resulting from so-called Treasury economy. Again, there is no one to formulate in advance a proper manufacturing programme with the least assurance that there will be the means available in order to carry it to a successful conclusion; even ironwork of a part-finished structure has been known to be denied the wherewithal for a coat of paint! The cast-iron system of closing the programme at the termination of each financial year without carry forward is destructive of good management. Thus the

GOVERNMENT v. PRIVATE MANUFACTURE. § 111

position of a Government factory is equivalent to that of an army with no Minister of War, no strategic scheme, and a capricious and fitful transport and supply. The larger institutions, such as dockyards, etc., represent a national interest of sufficient magnitude to escape some of the disadvantages of Government control, but here the circumstances are exceptional.

Manufacturing by private firms under contract, therefore, has considerable advantages; but even here the want of regularity in the placing out of orders is not conducive to high economy; a private firm, however, is able to work in one job with another, and execute a Government contract in lieu of other work for which there may happen to be a lull in the demand. This is especially the case in war time, when (as at the present moment) a large proportion of our engineering works and factories, having little demand for their regular products, are mainly occupied in turning out munitions of war. Whatever the state of preparedness may be before war is declared, it is almost certain that the needs of the country, whether for aeroplanes, guns, or other items of armament, will be increased many times during the period of hostilities. The employment of private enterprise under these conditions is clearly desirable, and may be looked upon as imperative.

Once admit the above, the propriety of widely utilising the ordinary manufacturing resources of the country during peace time follows as a corollary, for it is only by this means that these resources can be brought promptly into operation when the need arises. A firm which has once executed contracts for any given article is always in a better position than one to whom the work is new; this is true in any case, but is more especially so where the preparations for manufacture involve the duplication of gauges, tool outfits, etc.

§ 111 AIRCRAFT IN WARFARE.

When work is done by contract it is absolutely necessary that it should be first *standardised* in every detail. The rigid methods of gauging and viewing which have definitely to be adopted when aeroplanes (or other implements of war) are being manufactured to Government specification and contract, render anything in the way of ambiguity or alteration during manufacture intolerable. Therefore, whatever be the relative merits or demerits of private and Government manufacture, the former can only properly be resorted to for work which has passed its experimental stage, and has been finally standardised in every detail. This involves, in the case of anything so progressive as an aeroplane, that the Government will of necessity carry the manufacture of every new design up to a certain point; we may say up to that point at which it has become, after due tests and trials, an officially accepted type. This is almost exactly the position as it has come about: the Royal Aircraft Factory is directly responsible for the initial development of every new model (with the exception of some few "proprietary" types which have been taken into service): the only difficulty at present is that the resources of the factory are not sufficient fully to cope with even this preliminary work, and, in consequence, private enterprise is being called upon to do more than ought to be the case: the standardisation is having to be effected whilst manufacture is under weigh.

In view of the present position and the enormous development which may be anticipated in the course of the next few years, it will, in the author's opinion, be necessary very greatly to strengthen and increase the establishment of the Aircraft Factory in the near future.

§ 112. *Future Maintenance of British Supremacy. Continuity of Policy.* The supremacy of British aircraft can only be maintained by the adoption of a thoroughly

ROLE OF THE ROYAL AIRCRAFT FACTORY. § 112

progressive constructional policy, guided constantly by the most recent scientific discovery and research, and by utilising to the full information and experience gained in the Services. The day is past when technique or craftsmanship can be permanently bottled, and the trade or craft in question monopolised by any one nation, as was at one time the case. Under present-day conditions the lead can only be obtained and held by mobility and progress in which the motive power is derived by the combination of brains, energy, and material resources. The most that can be hoped is to obtain a lead of two or three years in advance of other nations, and to keep it. The task is not beyond the power of the country; we have both the men and the money, and an Empire whose preservation demands that nothing shall be left to chance.

The key to the whole situation lies in the proper organisation and control of the manufacturing resources of the Government, as at present represented by the Royal Aircraft Factory. This must be based on a clear conception of the duties of the factory as the birthplace of new types and the nursery for their development, also as the headquarters of full-scale experimental work, that is to say, tests and investigations engineering in character, or those in which actual flying is involved, as distinct from laboratory experiment. The deficiencies at present existing are due, firstly, to the fact that the Treasury has too much control over the Factory, and the Factory not enough control over the Treasury; secondly, there is no one upon whom definitely devolves the duty of initiating any departure in advance of immediate requirements; thirdly, the resources of the factory have been insufficient for the needs of the Services; it has been necessary to send out drawings and specifications to contractors before the designs have been standardised or even thoroughly established, with all the little attendant difficulties in the

§ 112   AIRCRAFT IN WARFARE.

matter of minor alterations, ambiguities as to gauging, etc.; also with the loss of any real pretentions to secrecy. Lastly, there is a tendency to divorce the aircraft development of the two Services—the Army and Navy; this the author considers to be bad. The main supplies of established types may certainly be obtained by the two Services from independent sources or from different contractors, but to separate the experimental or developmental phase of construction appears to have nothing to commend it.

The deficiencies of the present *régime*, such as they are, in no way reflect adversely on the existing staff and personnel of the Royal Aircraft Factory as it stands; in fact, it is undeniably greatly to the credit of all concerned that so much has been done. It is, however, hard to say who is supposed to be responsible for supplying initiative and foresight. That initiative has not been lacking is evident, but it is an open question whether anyone could have been accused of neglect of duty if the factory had never developed or constructed a solitary aeroplane.

Actually that which is lacking is something analogous to a directorate, a Board whose existence would ensure continuity of policy, and whose members would be definitely responsible for the sufficiency of the constructional programme so far as its developmental side is concerned, and for securing the needed Treasury support.

§ 113. *A Board of Aeronautical Construction.* The duties adumbrated in the preceding paragraph would be best deputed to a Board of Aeronautical Construction, in which both Army and Navy are represented by the responsible heads respectively of the two branches of the Arm—namely, the Director-General of Military Aeronautics and the Director of the Air Department of the Admiralty, in addition to a strong civilian contingent selected for their eminence or attainments in such

BOARD OF AERONAUTICAL CONSTRUCTION. § 113

directions as aeronautical or mechanical engineering, manufacturing, naval architecture, business management (organisation), finance, etc., and including the Superintendent of the Factory. In view of the fact that the future of the new Arm has yet to be determined, and in view of the vital importance of this future, it would seem desirable that certain Cabinet Ministers, such as the Minister of War and the First Lord of the Admiralty, should *ex officio* be members of the Board. This may possibly appear to be giving unnecessary importance to the idea, but it must be remembered that the existing Arms of the Services, during the earlier stages of their history, were considered of sufficient importance for the most minute and detailed attention of kings and princes, and the new Arm might almost claim as its right similar solicitude from those on whom the burden of office has fallen.

The duties and functions of the proposed Board would be in nowise limited to the aircraft themselves, but would extend to aircraft and counter-aircraft armament, and, further, to all questions of matériel ancillary to the employment of aircraft in the Services, including aeroplane vessels or ships.

The duties and constitution of the Advisory Committee for Aeronautics would remain as at present, being in no way affected. In some few cases it is possible that questions touching the work done at the Royal Aircraft Factory would be referred to the new Board in place of the Advisory Committee.

The arrangements regulating the Board in the matter of expenditure would need to be on a basis compatible with the responsibilities; a refusal or a cutting down by the Treasury of the requisitions by the Board, either annual or supplementary, should be rendered next to impossible. It would suffice for the purpose if, in case

§ 113   AIRCRAFT IN WARFARE.

of such eventuality, it were made incumbent upon the civilian section of the Board to resign *en bloc*. Parliament and the public would thus be advised that something had gone wrong with the "machine." To create this position it is only necessary for a public statement to be made by a responsible Minister of the Crown that the Board has at its disposal whatever funds it deems necessary; this is virtually the footing on which the present Advisory Committee is placed.[*]

The alternative to the creation of a Board, such as suggested in the present chapter, would be an extension of the powers of the Advisory Committee. The present functions of that Committee are strictly advisory; and they are, to all intents and purposes, confined to the scientific and technical side of the subject; the personnel of the Committee also has obviously been chosen on the basis of this being the intention. The Committee expends no money directly, but controls grants on account of aeronautics so far as relating to research work and the like. It would be impossible without destroying the whole intention and character of the Committee, to assign to it those duties in relation to the national programme of aeronautical construction for which the author is advocating the formation of a Board of Aeronautical Construction; hence any such change may be regarded as out of the question.

[*] House of Commons, May 5th, 1909

CHAPTER XVIII.

RETROSPECT. FURTHER NOTES ON THE *N-SQUARE* LAW. PARTIAL CONCENTRATION. AIR RAIDS: VALUE OF NUMBERS. STRATEGIC EMPLOYMENT OF AIR POWER.

§ 114. *Scope and Limitations of the Present Work.* In the present work it has been the author's endeavour to give an account of the existing position and the future possibilities of aircraft in its Military and Naval usage; in so far at least as present day knowledge permits of a reasoned forecast. There remains considerable ground however, to cover which no attempt has been made; thus we have the whole subject of aeronautical photography in its present relation on which much might have been said; also many quasi-technical questions connected with aeronautical signalling, by wireless and otherwise, might legitimately have been introduced. Beyond this the whole subject of aeroplane design, as affected by the various kinds of usage in warfare, is itself one of vast and intricate interest,—this has been barely touched upon. In these matters considerations of secrecy have necessitated reticence; the author had obviously to steer clear of much that was known to him on the subject of our aeronautical equipment, and to confine himself for his facts to such material as was common property before the date of hostilities, or had become so since. As an indication that the position has not been without difficulty, it may perhaps be mentioned that (contrary to what might be expected) it is not always permissible to reproduce matter which has

§ 114   AIRCRAFT IN WARFARE.

already been published in the press; should it thus appear that the author has not taken full advantage of material already published elsewhere, it will be fair that he should be credited with an adequate reason. Certain digressions from the main subject have on the other hand been made, and here and there speculative incursions into the unknown have been ventured. The most important digression is without question that constituting the subject matter of Chapters V. and VI., involving the demonstration of the *n-square* law. The author believes that this law will, in due course, be recognised as fundamental even in relation to ordinary military operations where its application is commonly masked by conditions extraneous to the hypothesis. Still more readily will its importance be recognised in Naval warfare, as already exemplified by the Battle of Trafalgar.* The clearest and cleanest application of the law, however, will unquestionably be in connection with aerial warfare, here the author predicts that, other things being equal, it will be found to operate with almost mathematical precision.

§ 115. *The n-square law as affected by the Technique of Gunnery.* In the application of the principle of concentration and the *n-square* law to Naval warfare under modern conditions, a difficulty occurs which has not so far been adequately dealt with, and which is worthy of full discussion. This difficulty mainly concerns existent methods of range finding, and is to the effect that when the fire of more than one vessel is brought to bear on a single ship of the enemy, the same accuracy— as evidenced by the percentage of hits—is not attainable as in ship-to-ship combat.

It is to be understood that after the range has been found as accurately as possible by the instrument known

* Chapter VI. §§ 40, 41 and 42.

THE N² LAW AND GUNNERY TECHNIQUE. § 115

as a *range-finder*, the final corrections are made by firing salvos, each salvo being observed, and an appropriate correction given. When the range has been thus determined, firing by salvos may be discontinued and independent firing resorted to, the main advantage of the latter being an increased rapidity of fire. If it be observed that the firing is becoming wild, that is to say, if the range has been lost, firing by salvos may be resumed.

The objection to more than one battleship making a target of a single vessel of the enemy is that it is difficult to avoid uncertainty as to whose projectiles are going wild, and so when independent fire is the order of the day, it is impossible for the gunnery officer to tell whether his own gunners have lost the range or whether the bad shooting is from the co-operating vessel. It then becomes necessary for both ships in turn to resort to salvo firing, in order to check their range and correct their aim, and thus at the best the speed of fire is unavoidably reduced at intervals during an engagement.

The objection no doubt is valid, but, like other objections, the question is one of degree. The loss of speed of fire when salvo firing is adopted depends to a great extent upon the type of vessel, and more especially upon the armament. Thus if the vessel be one of the pre-dreadnought period having in its primary armament guns of various calibre and of different rapidity of fire, it is clear that in salvo firing the lighter guns (also the more rapid) either will not be employed or will have their speed of fire regulated by that of the guns of heavier calibre. In the case however, of the all-big-gun ship—as dating from the original "Dreadnought"—the loss is not so great, and the objection of proportionately less weight.

It is to be remembered that at modern ranges, some-

§ 115   AIRCRAFT IN WARFARE.

times amounting to a distance of 8 or 10 miles between opposed fleets,* the time of flight of the projectiles is very great. It may amount to some 20 or 30 seconds, and thus if two vessels are concentrating their fire on one of the enemy and firing by salvos, it will frequently be the case that two salvos of projectiles are in flight at the same time, and the uninitiated would not be certain which salvo belongs to which vessel: for the professional gunner however, the matter is different. Although the correct range may not be known or may be wrongly determined in the first instance, the gunner, or the officer responsible for the control, knows precisely the range for which he has set his elevation, and consequently he knows to a fraction of a second the interval which will elapse between the discharge of the salvo and the time the projectiles strike the water; thus unless two salvos are actually fired to strike the water within say a second of one another there will be no reasonable doubt which is which.

It may fairly be urged that the troubles of observation and of gun fire direction in naval actions tend to increase, and at the best the conditions are already sufficiently exacting. It is, for instance, not uncommon when combatant vessels are separated by some 8 or 10 miles, for destroyers and torpedo boats to be told off to create clouds of smoke, by which the difficulties of observation may be indefinitely increased. It is probable, in fact it is almost certain, that in the future the aeroplane will come to the rescue of naval gunnery, just as it is already employed in co-operation with long range artillery on land. The author believes that in future naval warfare much of the observation work and fire control will be corrected by aircraft, either dirigible or aeroplane being used; under these conditions it will be necessary

* Perhaps even 12 miles as a maximum estimate; so far battle experience is lacking. The 4 or 5 miles given in § 36 is (from the context) an ordinary minimum.

THE N^2 LAW AND GUNNERY TECHNIQUE.   § 115

for the battleship to notify to its associated aircraft the range of each salvo, so that when the fire of two or more vessels is concentrated on one, the aerial observer will be able to locate the position of any given salvo with certainty. There are many ways in which this might in effect be accomplished; for example, a smoke or flash signal could be fired on board the battleship at a pre-arranged one or two seconds' interval before the salvo is due to strike the water. The observer or airman will note the said signal and pick out the corresponding salvo from the splashes of independent fire or of salvos from other vessels, signalling in reply whether too short, too long, or right, or left, according to a pre-arranged code.

It will be quite clear from the foregoing discussion that although undoubtedly two or three ships concentrating their fire on one of the enemy may be detrimental to accurate shooting, the difficulties are such as can be met, and that with only a moderate loss of fire efficiency. Now, if the advantage shown to accrue from fire concentration, as exemplified by the *n-square* law, were something trifling or negligible, in comparison with the difficulties involved, then, without doubt, it might be judged that in practice the ship-to-ship combat would be the best, even when a numerical superiority exists. But the advantage of concentration as exemplified by the *n-square* law is not negligible or trifling, it is overwhelming, and of such a character as to entirely outweigh any objections which can be raised from the gunnery standpoint.[*] In brief, the controversy (so far as it is so) is a conflict between a fundamental principle and a matter

[*] Discussing the present subject with the author, a Naval officer of high rank not only expressed the opinion that the concentration of the fire of two ships on one is impracticable under modern conditions, but further stated that if he were fighting two ships against two ships of an enemy, he would *bring one of his ships into action first*, and only throw the other into the fight when the fire control mechanism of the enemy, *i.e.*, observation and fighting tops, telephones, etc., had been carried away or disabled. This view is the opposite extreme to that held and advocated by the author. In any case it is not thus that Nelson fought.

§ 115   AIRCRAFT IN WARFARE.

of technique, and we know that in all cases when such a conflict takes place, it is the technique which has to adapt itself to meet the fundamentally important condition. The technique in the present case is the technique of. gunnery and fire control, and the author believes that it cannot be put too strongly that it is " up to " the gunnery officer (whenever possible) to carry into practice the concentration of the larger force on the lesser and to adapt his methods, cost what it may, to meet the requirements of the case; he cannot afford to flout a fundamental principle for the sake of simplifying the technique of his profession.

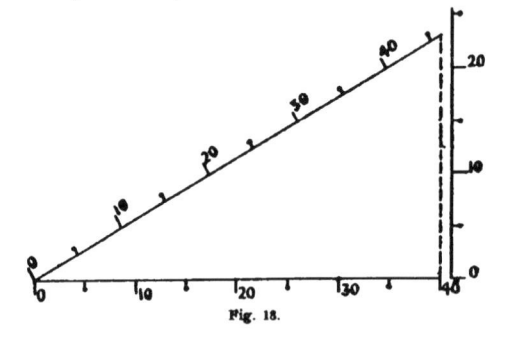

Fig. 18.

§ 116. *The n-square law and Partial Concentration.* In § 42 it was shown that if the whole of the "combined" fleet of 46 ships had been concentrated upon the British 40 ships the annihilation of the latter would have been complete, leaving the combined fleet victors with the equivalent of 23 whole ships to the good; this is now represented graphically in Fig. 18. By inadvertence this was referred to (quoting Villeneuve) as "the usage of former days." This is not strictly accurate, at least it requires qualification.

According to the said "usage of former days" 34 of the British vessels would have been opposed

182

THE N^2 LAW. PARTIAL CONCENTRATION. § 116

to 34 of the enemy ship to ship, and the remaining 6 British would have been opposed to 12 of the enemy, these conditions are represented graphically in Fig. 19. Thus it will be seen that the numerical surplus is reduced to 10.4 ships, the case being one of partial concentration. Of course in actuality the scheme, however carefully planned, would never result in the perfectly well ordered doubling of the excess of one fleet on the rear ships of the other; the construction, however, given in Fig. 19 is quite elastic, and any departure may be readily dealt with. Thus Fig. 19 may be taken as the

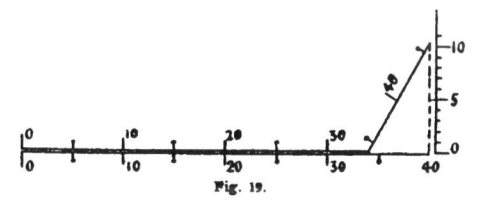

Fig. 19.

appropriate general graphic construction for the representation of any case of *partial concentration* in accordance with the *n-square* law.

It is worthy of remark that in cases of partial concentration there may always be a second or after phase in the battle when the residue of the superior force concentrated on the "tail" of the enemy having done its work, will throw its weight into the main combat, the final conditions will then be more nearly the same as if the initial concentration had been complete, as assumed in § 42.

§ 117. *Air Raids: The Value of Numbers.* The importance of numbers in duties other than actual fighting does not, generally speaking, follow the *n-square* law; it is nevertheless by no means negligible.

The reason here is that the object attacked is, ordinarily speaking, not an actively hostile force. Thus

§ 117   AIRCRAFT IN WARFARE.

even where, as in the attack on an arsenal or magazine, the position is protected by counter aircraft artillery, it is fair to assume that the latter is mounted at a sufficient distance from the main object of attack not to be endangered unless bombs are wilfully diverted from their objective. Under these conditions a numerically great attacking force of aeroplanes will manifestly possess an advantage in that they will divide the limited fire capacity of the defending batteries and so suffer less individual punishment; we may take it that the actual injury inflicted on the attacking fleet will be constant and independent of its numerical strength. If, by the nature of the attack, the period during which the air fleet is under fire is lessened by a numerical increase, there is a gain to an extent proportional to the reduction of time the defending batteries can be brought to bear.

In any case the gain is clear, as for example if 10 machines can do in a given time 10 times the mischief of one machine, and if this is done at the same average total loss it is done 10 times as economically. In other words, if a given weight of bombs have to be dropped and this be done by 10 separately attacking aeroplanes, the protecting batteries will be able to "get off" a 10 times greater number of shells than if the attack were planned and executed by the 10 machines simultaneously.

It is of some interest to remark that in § 64 (originally published Nov. 6th, 1914) the suggestion is made of an attack by a "few squadrons" of aeroplanes as constituting a reasonably effective concentration; this is an almost exact forecast of the practice as it obtains to-day, since a "Squadron" may be taken as from 16 to 20 machines and in recent air raids it is reported that about 60 or 70 machines have been employed. We may confidently look to a substantial numerical increase in the air raids of the future.

The author is inclined to believe that the tendency of the future will be towards machines of not too great size each dropping a comparatively few bombs, possibly no more than one large bomb being carried by each machine. This conclusion arises as a deduction from the fact that when machines are acting in great numbers it will not be possible (neither will it be politic) for any given machine to pass more than once over the object of attack, hence if a large number of bombs be carried they will need to be released almost simultaneously. Under these conditions a single large bomb of equal weight will possess a far greater potential capacity of destruction.

§ 118. *Aircraft v. Submarine.* Discussing the value of Aircraft as countering submarine activity in Chapter XI., the subject has perhaps been handled too much in detail, and some of the broader considerations have not been given sufficient prominence. It is not to be supposed that it will always be found possible on locating a submarine, to follow it up and immediately effect its destruction, since in the turbid waters of the Channel and parts of the North Sea (especially in rough weather) a submarine, by diving deeply and steering by gyro-compass, could frequently effect its escape. Quite apart from the method of attack it is the author's view that with a sufficiently numerous air reconnaissance, the enemy submarine will be subject to continuous and unremitting pressure to such an extent that, even where it may escape destruction, it will commonly fail in its object. Thus, taking the case of the large submarine having a great radius of action, it is impossible to make a long passage such as an incursion into the Atlantic from the Heligoland Bight round Cape Wrath, without steaming on the surface for a consider-

§ 118   AIRCRAFT IN WARFARE.

able proportion of the distance. Under these conditions, once located by an efficient air scout service, it will be tracked from day to day if need be, and, sooner or later, either by aircraft or destroyer, it will be brought to book. It is not suggested that under no circumstances could a submarine escape, it would, however, only do so by radically altering its course or by some other manœuvre involving the temporary abandonment of its purpose; ultimately the influence of aircraft on the high seas will be to keep the submarine submerged, under which condition its radius of action is greatly circumscribed. Thus persecuted, it will be reduced to surface running by night, and even then, unless favoured by the elements, will be liable to attack by fast light cruisers or destroyers which will be informed with considerable exactitude as to the whereabouts of their quarry.

Beyond the above, a submarine or submarines tracked by aircraft will have great difficulty in keeping a prearranged rendezvous, and any "neutral" vessel or fishing craft used for fuel supply and revictualling will be far more liable to detection than is at present the case.

The author believes that it is by continuous pressure of this kind, backed up by direct attack when occasion serves, that submarine activity will eventually be curbed. It has already been pointed out that the capacity of aircraft to warn merchantmen of danger will alone be sufficient to render the submarine threat quite ineffective, apart from any question of destroying the craft themselves.

Such work as contemplated can only be effectively performed by aircraft if sufficiently numerous, operating in units of flights or squadrons. It will be found comparatively useless to endeavour to carry out the duties in question by single machines, since it will often be necessary to sweep considerable areas of the ocean in

STRATEGIC EMPLOYMENT OF AIR POWER. § 118

order to pick up the trail or get on the track of a submarine that has been temporarily lost. It is thus only when the number of machines and the organisation is sufficiently developed that the power of aircraft as controlling submarine activity will be fully realised.

§ 119. *The Strategic Employment of Aircraft on a Large Scale.* It is becoming more and more clear as time goes by that the future of Aircraft in Warfare is a subject of such vast potentiality that we may to-day consider ourselves only on the outer fringe of developments destined ultimately to carry us far beyond anything yet conceived. We are at present only on the threshold of a revolution which aircraft will ultimately bring about in the conduct of warfare.

Thus, in the existing phase of the present war, were our aircraft of sufficient numerical strength, it would no longer be a matter of individual and isolated raids on selected places at which the maximum of injury could be inflicted, but rather a continuous and unrelenting attack on each and every point of strategic importance. Depôts of every kind in the rear of the enemy's lines would cease to exist; rolling stock and mechanical transport would be destroyed; no bridge would be allowed to stand for 24 hours; railway junctions would be subject to continuous bombardment, and the lines of railway and roads themselves broken up daily by giant bombs to such an extent as to baffle all attempts to maintain or restore communication.

In this manner a virtually impassable zone would be created in the rear of the enemy's defences, a zone varying, perhaps, from 100 to 200 miles in width. Once this condition has been brought about, the position of the defending force must be considered as precarious; not only will the defence be slowly strangled from the uncertainty and lack of supplies of all kinds, but ultimately retreat will become impossible. The defending

§ 119   AIRCRAFT IN WARFARE.

force will find itself literally in a state of siege under the worst possible conditions, for the position will be one in the form of an extended line along which the forces of all arms will be definitely immobilised, for the lateral communications will suffer no less than the lines from the rear. Such a position of affairs presents all the elements conducive to complete and irreparable disaster.

Thus, in the extended employment of aircraft, we have the means at hand of compelling a bloodless victory; for, once admit the truth of the present conclusions, the serious and comprehensive threatening of the communications of the enemy by aircraft on the lines indicated can only be answered by his retirement. If he neglects to take this step until too late, he pays the penalty in annihilation or surrender; the matter thus stated becomes one involving the ordinary logic of military necessity.

The magnitude of the aeronautical forces and establishment necessary to effect the present purpose must not be under-estimated. In order to prove a decisive factor the *devastated zone* will need to be of very great area, a belt of from 50 to 100 miles in width probably represents the minimum, and the destruction wrought over the said zone must be complete and thorough in every important respect. The accomplishment, however, is commensurate with the magnitude of the means, for an operation on the scale stated must be met by the enemy by a withdrawal of corresponding magnitude ; no ordinary retreat of a few miles to a second line of defence can avail him. From the time his aircraft and air defences are overpowered and his communications placed in jeopardy, he must prepare to fall back on new lines established beyond the zone of devastation, that is to say, if the work is effectively done his retirement can be but little short of 50 or 100 miles. In the present war, this would mean virtually the evacuation and abandonment of the

STRATEGIC EMPLOYMENT OF AIR POWER. § 119

whole of the allied territory at present occupied in Flanders and in the North and West of France. Once the captured territory has been organised and the necessary preparations have been made, the attack would be repeated, and, presuming the continued supremacy of our air fleets. no resistance or defence by the enemy of a permanent character can be sustained.

CHAPTER XIX.

UNSOLVED QUESTIONS OF NATIONAL DEFENCE. RADIUS OF ACTION AND POWER OF AGGRESSION. INTER-DEPENDENCE OF NAVAL AND AIR DEFENCE. AERONAUTICAL DEVELOPMENT A NATIONAL RESPONSIBILITY. IMMEDIATE MEASURES ADVOCATED.

§ 120. *National Defence. Air Raids.* In considering the more far-reaching effects of Aircraft in Warfare, it is more than ever necessary that we should substitute in our minds for what we may see to-day, a picture of what may reasonably be expected in the not very distant future. Thus from the military standpoint and even from the standpoint of the Nation, the effect of the raids by German aircraft has been a negligble quantity; it has moreover cost the enemy no small expenditure of energy (which he can ill afford to squander) to effect this relatively microscopic injury. Tersely put, air-raids on Great Britain by Zeppelin do not pay. We have no reason, however, to assume that this condition of affairs will last; on the contrary, we must make provision against future possibilities, when air-raids will be conducted in so effective a manner that, if not successfully opposed and beaten back, they *will* pay.

§ 121. *The Defence of London.* A broad question at once arises: will it be possible in the future to entirely and effectively defend from aerial attack a city of the size of London situated within so short a distance of the enemy's frontiers? For the purposes of the proposition we must assume the whole of the continental coastline as hostile territory; on this basis the distance is no more than one hour's flight.

THE DEFENCE OF LONDON. § 121

There is no doubt that so long as the weather conditions are favourable to defence, anything in the nature of a daylight attack on London could be rendered impossible by a sufficient defending force of aeroplanes, but here even, in the event of an attack in great force, it is by no means certain that some measure of success might not be achieved; it would at least require an immense preponderance of power, if every hostile aeroplane is to be beaten back or otherwise accounted for.

When, however, the weather conditions are favourable to attack, also in the case of attack by night, there is no means of defence at present known to the author which would prevent the enemy from inflicting enormous damage if he attack in sufficient numerical force and is prepared to act with determination in spite of any losses he may sustain; no reasonable superiority in the defending aircraft, either individually or numerically, can be entirely effective. Neither can we pin our faith to counter-aircraft artillery; under the conditions in question it may prove to be useless.

We have so far not witnessed an attack by aircraft on an important city on a grand scale, such as, without doubt, the future has in store. The "raids" which have hitherto been carried out are quite trivial and ineffective affairs compared with what in due course will become possible. The critical point, and the point to be aimed at as an act of war, is that at which the fire-extinguishing appliances of the community are beaten or overcome. Up to this point the damage done may be taken as roughly proportional to the means and cost of its accomplishment; beyond that point the damage is disproportionately great: the city may be destroyed *in toto*.

There will always be the sentimentalist who has implicit faith (in spite of experience) in the omnipotence of peace conferences and the like and the unalienable

§ 121   AIRCRAFT IN WARFARE.

rights of humanity, who will decline to believe that after the present war Nation will need to defend itself against Nation by brute force. To these the destruction of a city of 5,000,000 peaceable inhabitants by fire with the scenes of horror that would inevitably ensue, will be looked upon as the figment of a diseased imagination, to these the author does not address himself;* he regards the possibility as one which it behoves us to consider and meet as a matter of ordinary military precaution, not regarding it as any more improbable or unexpected than any other hostile act of which an enemy might be capable.

§ 122. *Justification for Attack upon Capital City.* It is futile to attempt to disguise the self-evident fact that a serious attack on the capital city of an enemy, containing in its heart the administrative centre both of his Army and Navy, in addition to the headquarters of his Government, cannot be regarded other than as a legitimate act of warfare. No international agreement or convention can make it otherwise. Once war is declared the successful waging of war becomes the first duty of a belligerent Government, it obviously cannot do or countenance any act, or the neglect of any act, which could by any possibility compromise the issue, without thereby proving false to its trust. There is really no escape from this. Unquestionably, the destruction of a capital city such as London, with the administrative centres aforesaid, would be a military achievement of the first order of magnitude ; it would be, from an enemy standpoint, an achievement of far greater potential value than any ordinary success or victory in the field of battle.

We may then disabuse our minds of the popular notion that the raiding or attacking of London by aircraft is to be regarded as something contrary to the

*A certain cynic once defined a fool as a man who could *only* learn by experience. The author prefers the more benevolent definition that a fool is one to whom the teaching of experience is of no avail.

ATTACK ON CAPITAL CITY. § 122

established ethics of warfare; we recognise that we are, in the protection of our capital, face to face with a necessary problem of national defence of the first magnitude. Let us admit that, given a determined enemy in the possession of the French and Belgian littoral, the problem in future will be increasingly difficult. Let us go further, and, for the purpose of argument, assume that it may become impossible. We have no assurance in all the circumstances that this is not the truth. What then will be the measures by which the new situation can be met? It is wholesome to consider the position on this basis.

§ 123. *The Incentive to Attack. The Real Source of Weakness.* It is evident that if the administrative headquarters of the Army and Navy were removed to some less accessible position, and in fact if London were to cease to be the centre of Government, the main incentive to attack, as a military operation, would be destroyed, and the danger in question disposed of. Obviously London as a city would be no less vulnerable than before, and it would be open to be wantonly raided unless adequate means of defence were provided. Measures of defence, however, to be effective have always to be proportioned to the incentive to attack, and to reduce the incentive to a minimum is to make the most of such means of protection as are available. Putting this in other words, we have it that the enemy would not be prepared to pay so high a price or take the same risks for the privilege of destroying private property and murdering civilians, as he would if he were able at the same stroke to disorganize the whole administrative machinery of the State. Also, so long as any act of aggression has admittedly no military value, it may be answered by appropriate reprisal.*

---

*A reprisal to be effective must be delivered with promptitude like the *riposte* of a skilled fencer. A reprisal which is too long delayed possesses no moral weight and has every appearance of an independent act of aggression; it may even plausibly

§ 123   AIRCRAFT IN WARFARE.

The possible need for abandoning the present capital as the centre of administration in wartime carries with it as a corollary its abandonment equally in time of peace, at least so far as the control of the Army and Navy is concerned ; since, on the declaration of war, or even without a formal declaration, the aircraft of the enemy may already be mobilised for an attack. Of course our premises are hypothetical, we have no proof yet that the adequate defence of London from hostile aircraft will actually become impossible, but equally it is clear that the contingency may have to be faced, and therefore it is one that must be taken seriously.

§ 124. *The Question of Fire Risk.* Apart from the active defence provided by a numerically strong and vigilant air fleet, the most important factor in the protection of a city from hostile aircraft is to be sought in the prevention of fire. Thus a city in which fire-proof or fire-resisting construction is extensively employed, and in which a town-planning scheme has been adopted with a view to the localisation of any conflagration that may get out of hand, will be far safer and more easily defended than one in which these precautions are not taken. It goes without saying that all the usual appliances for dealing with the outbreak of fire should be liberally provided in any case. The greater and more thorough the precautions, the less probability will there be of the enemy attack being successful, and the larger the scale on which it will have to be conducted to have any hope of success; conversely the easier will be rendered the effective defence. It is to be understood that the word *success* as here used is measured by whether or no the extent of

be given as an excuse for a subsequent repetition of the original offence. It is thus detrimental to the cause of humanity to tie the hands of a belligerent by inter national convention. Such conventions result in delays whilst law officers are consulted and whilst committees are called and decisions are reached , also they result in no preparations being made for counter measures such as comprehended by the word reprisal. The power of reprisal and the knowledge that the means of reprisal exists will ever be a far greater deterrent than any pseudo-legal document

AIR RAIDS: EFFECTIVE RADIUS.   § 124

direct injury is sufficient to cause a general conflagration, as already laid down.

§ 125. *The Question of Radius of Action.* A point of great importance in the present connection is the radius of action of the aircraft by which attacks such as under discussion will be carried out. Evidently it is the aeroplane or flying machine which chiefly concerns us, and due allowance for possible improvement over existing performance must be admitted.

When we are discussing the range or radius of action of a battleship or cruiser we are dealing with something definite, such vessel can either reach a given destination with its power of aggression unimpaired, or it cannot get there at all; not so with the aeroplane. In the aeroplane the power of aggression and the range or radius of action are alternative quantities, which, measured by the *weight* of bombs and the *weight* of fuel (*i.e.*, petrol) respectively, represent a definite amount in sum. Thus if one-third of the maximum gross weight of the machine be taken to represent its combined petrol and bomb capacity, the maximum distance which can be flown by an aeroplane is about 1,200 miles, or 600 out and home, if the whole of the said capacity be devoted to petrol. When part of the capacity is devoted to the carrying of bombs the range of flight is proportionately lowered, so that the position of affairs may be represented as in Fig. 20, in which it will be seen that as the range of flight is increased the value of the machine for the purposes of attack is diminished till at a maximum out-and-home radius of 600 miles it falls to zero: the machine has ceased to be capable of offence.

It is not only in its power of offence that the long-distance aeroplane is at a military disadvantage; it is so in respect of all other attributes which are involved in the problem of weight. For example, any machine built

§ 125 AIRCRAFT IN WARFARE.

expressly for long distance raiding, will be essentially a relatively slow machine, since speed means engine weight; it must be, comparatively speaking, a relatively poor climber for the same reason. Again, it cannot afford to carry shield or armour, neither can weight be spared for a defensive gun armament. All these facts mean that as the distance to be raided becomes greater, defence will become more and more easy, and point to the conclusion that in actual warfare the maximum distance which can be effectively raided by aeroplane will be far less than the theoretical maximum aforesaid. Beyond this the opportunities for defensive counter

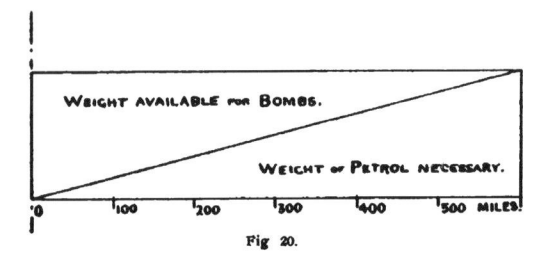

Fig 20.

measures become greater, and the possibility of taking advantage of favourable weather conditions less, the greater the distance involved in the raid. Taking everything into account, the author thinks it improbable that raids over territory held by an enemy exceeding 300 or 400 miles will be found practicable, and in the face of opposition it would be rare for an attempt of this magnitude to succeed unless conducted by a force of overwhelming numerical strength.

§ 126. *The Danger to Aircraft Factories and Production*. There is a further point in respect of which the position of aircraft is without exact parallel in the other arms of the Services; in a war of any magnitude or duration the manufacture during the period of hos-

DEFENCE OF AIRCRAFT FACTORIES. § 126

tilities is vital to the maintenance of the Arm at its initial strength, and the manufacture is itself threatened if the enemy once obtain, aeronautically, the upper hand. Thus the life of an aeroplane in active service is a matter of only some three or four months, and the manufacturing resources of the country must thus be capable of replacing the whole active force of aeroplanes three or four times over in every year. On the other hand, our sources of supply, or those situated within raiding distance of hostile territory, would be seriously imperilled were the enemy to obtain, even for a short time, a sufficient preponderance of air power. The intention of thus making use of aeronautical ascendency to extinguish the enemy's sources of supply has been clearly manifested in the present war, as witness the raids executed against Friedrichshaven and other Zeppelin bases; the reason that such tactics have not been pushed to the extreme and followed to their logical conclusion is clearly that the raiding aeroplane, in respect of type, numerical strength, and organisation, is yet in its infancy.

For the above reason it is the author's opinion that the main aeronautical manufacturing resources of any country will eventually be established out of effective reach of hostile territory; in the case of Great Britain this indicates the selection of a position some three or four hundred miles from the continental littoral. The circumstances point ultimately to the industrial districts of Belfast and the Clyde, as appropriate centres for the production of both aeroplanes and so-called "seaplanes" in the quantities the future will demand. Such a position is out of range of existing hostile aircraft, and will probably remain so for many years to come. Looking beyond this it is a position giving such great possibilities of defence, that so long as we assume the motive power engine subject

§ 126   AIRCRAFT IN WARFARE.

to its known restrictions as a form of heat engine, it may be regarded as safe for all time. The position of Belfast is such that, even if we assume the whole Netherlands, Belgium and the French littoral to be in the hands of an enemy, the distance to be flown is approximately 400 miles,[*] during almost the whole of which distance enemy aircraft will have to run the gauntlet of our air defence, both aeroplane and counter aircraft artillery.

§ 127. *Comparison with Navy.* It is true that the Aeronautical Arm is not alone in requiring manufacturing facilities during the period of hostilities, and in being liable to the dislocation of these facilities *by its own kind*. The same is true, but in far less degree, of the Navy; in the latter these facilities (in the form of our Naval building yards and dockyards) are quite essential to the proper upkeep of the Fleet, although the amount of new construction (in comparison with aircraft) is relatively small. It is nevertheless regarded by the Naval authorities as essential that our dockyards, etc., shall be so placed as to be capable of effective defence against naval raids, and any situation which cannot be made to comply with this condition has sooner or later to be abandoned, or at least new bases have to be created to take over its more important functions. The position of the Aeronautical Arm, however, is unique in the relatively great importance of the daily output of new machines, and in the relative ease with which this may be interfered with by enemy enterprise if due precautions are not taken. Thus the present recommendation may be regarded as the extension of a principle, admitted in the selection for the site of a ship-building yard or dockyard, to the choice of a headquarters for aeronautical construction.

It is extremely doubtful whether we shall witness

[*] Compare Appendix II. In the present war the position is far more favourable; the Midlands and West of England are reasonably safe from attack.

during the present war raids extending to anything approaching 300 or 400 miles out and home over enemy territory, so that the recommendation suggested above is probably more drastic than necessitated by present conditions; however, all depends upon the duration of the war, the technical difficulties in the way of the production of suitable machines can be surmounted at any time without great difficulty. Beyond this there is no reason to suppose that during the present war the French littoral will be in other than friendly hands, whereas in the foregoing discussion the broader basis has been assumed, namely, that all territory not actually British must be considered as potentially hostile.

§ 128. *Air Raids and the Naval Outlook.* The possibility of air raids on a large scale on the Naval outlook will certainly be far-reaching in its effects. All depôts, dockyards, etc., within easy range of alien territory, such as those situated on our southern coast, can no longer be regarded as secure from bombardment; the defence of such places as Portsmouth and Devonport from attack by air may prove an almost if not quite impossible proposition; the weather conditions may be such as to let the enemy through even in face of a numerically superior defensive force. Thus it may be confidently anticipated that these southern depôts will become points of subsidiary importance, useful enough in times of European peace, but forming no really essential part of the scheme of National defence in the event of a great European war. The "centre of gravity" of the bases on which the Navy will rely for its support is bound to move northward and still further north as the power of the aeronautical Arm is uncoiled, and eventually the strategic centre of our defences, both Naval and Aeronautical, will perforce be located in the region of the Irish Sea and North Channel; it will then be in the neighbourhood of Belfast on the one

§ 128   AIRCRAFT IN WARFARE.

hand and the Clyde on the other, that our main Naval building yards, dockyards and important depôts will be established, and our largest and most important aircraft factories will be installed.

If the above conclusions are sound it may be found necessary, for reasons of Naval strategy, to cut a ship canal through from the Clyde to the river Forth. This would be an engineering feat of considerable magnitude, involving, besides the actual cutting itself, the deepening of the Clyde for a distance of some 12 or more miles between Clydebank and Greenock, in addition to extensive dredging of the River Forth. The existing Forth and Clyde Canal is an ordinary inland navigation, with numerous locks, fit only for lighters or barges of length not exceeding 68 feet. The height of the "divide" is about 160 feet.

A real ship canal for the purpose intended—to be navigable by the largest of our battleships—would be an undertaking of the same order of magnitude as the Kaiser Wilhelm or Kiel Canal, and we may assume would involve an expenditure probably not less than forty millions sterling. Such a canal would bring the Naval base at Rosyth within a few hours steaming of the Clyde, or roughly within twelve hours of Belfast Lough.

§ 129. *Aeronautical and Naval Defence indissolubly associated.* It is evident that the whole scheme for aeronautical defence must and will be closely related to the distribution of our Naval bases. In fact it is our Navy and defensive aircraft which henceforward will jointly constitute Britain's first line of defence. It is for this reason that the control of our defending air forces falls naturally to the Admiralty rather than the War Office. The most important objectives of an enemy air-raid, apart from attack on our centre of government, will be without doubt our Battle Squadrons, our Naval bases and

FUTURE OF AERONAUTICAL ARM.   § 129

dockyards, and our aircraft and shipping centres, for it is here that, apart from any question of invasion, Great Britain is most vulnerable. The problem of giving adequate protection to these is manifestly a work which only the Admiralty is competent to undertake. As already pointed out there are geographic positions which in no way lend themselves to aeronautical defence, it will be incumbent upon the Naval Authorities to determine when and under what conditions these will need to be abandoned. Generally speaking, a point can only be defended from hostile aircraft when its approach necessitates a considerable length of flight over British territory. Alternatively a point may also be considered defendable if the total distance from hostile territory is sufficient, *provided that the intervening sea is effectively patrolled;* thus again the intimate relation of aeronautical to naval defence becomes manifest.

§ 130. *The Future of the Aeronautical Arm a National Question.* It is more than probable that before the termination of the present war we may witness and experience aerial raids on a scale immeasurably greater than anything so far attempted, either by the enemy or by our own airmen; it is also probable that the strategic employment of the aeronautical Arm on the lines laid down in the preceding chapter (§ 119) will become a *fait accompli.* The extent of realisation depends upon the duration of the war and the numerical strength of the airfleets which will become available before the conclusion of hostilities.

In the author's opinion it is vitally necessary, both with a view to ensuring speedy victory and to our future as a nation, that our manufacturing resources in the production of aircraft should be developed to the utmost; aeroplanes and still more aeroplanes will be needed, aeroplanes in the maximum possible quantities of every useful

§ 130   AIRCRAFT IN WARFARE.

type, whether reconnaissance, bomb-dropping, or fighting machines; our total present capacity for production is petty in comparison with what we have evidence the future will demand.

The question of the future of the Aeronautical Arm is not purely the concern of the Army and Navy, it cuts deeper; it is essentially an affair of the Nation. It is national because it concerns both Services. It is national because it is of wider and more far-reaching moment than comprised by its relation to either. It is national because it depends upon our national industrial resources, and may tax these to the uttermost; national because it is the Arm of greatest potential development in the present war, and in future warfare may decide the fate of Nations. Finally, it is national because it is the Arm which will have to be ever ready, ever mobilised, both in time of peace and war: it is the Arm which in the warfare of the future may act with decisive effect within a few hours of the outbreak of hostilities.

§ 131. *In Conclusion.* That we have temporarily the upper hand in military aeronautics there is no doubt, but this is due more to our technical prescience than to the scale or magnitude of our national preparedness. In other words, our present lead is only in part due to our own effort, it is largely due to the mistake made by the enemy prior to the war in devoting altogether disproportionate attention to the large dirigibles: Germany backed the wrong horse. The Zeppelin, from the military standpoint, has proved a complete failure. If the resources thus diverted into a useless channel had been devoted to the development of the aeroplane and strengthening of the enemy flying corps, the position from our point of view might have been nowise so satisfactory. Having been thus favoured with the advantage by what may almost be regarded as a

IN CONCLUSION. § 131

"chance of war," we must make up our minds to maintain it by any and every means in our power.

Let us not delude ourselves by supposing that the enemy will be content to allow us to retain our advantage without a keenly contested struggle; he is probably ere this fully alive to his past mistake, and will strain every nerve to rectify matters; there is already evidence of strenuous effort in that direction. The chief factor in the coming contest in aeronautical armament will undoubtedly prove to be the relative manufacturing resources available respectively to the two belligerent groups; here Great Britain and her Allies have an undoubted advantage.

In concluding the present work, the author claims that a clear case has been made out for an immediate and thoroughgoing overhaul of our programme and administration as touching the future of the Aeronautical Arm, and to this end urges for immediate consideration the following:—

(1) That in view of the potentialities of the Aeronautical Arm, a comprehensive scheme of construction should be forthwith prepared, in which provision shall be made for organizing, utilizing, and developing every available source of manufacture and supply.

(2) That if possible certain of our present types of aeroplane be virtually adopted "for the duration of the war," and existing manufacturing facilities should be utilised for their uninterrupted production to the utmost of their capacity.*

(3) That where it is decided that new types are required, new sources of production should so far as possible be tapped or new works equipped, in order that

* A given type of aeroplane may not be the best we know how to make, but the same may be said of our small arms, or our field pieces, it does its work, however, and is understood by the men who handle it in the field: these are points worth a great deal. It is not realised by those who are not intimately connected with manufacture the extent to which alterations or improvements during quantity manufacture are detrimental to output, especially is this the case when working at high pressure Fixity of design should be looked upon as a *sine qua non* once manufacture has been embarked upon.

§ 131   AIRCRAFT IN WARFARE.

output should not be made to suffer. In other words, the policy should tend in the direction of establishing each new type with the factory for its production as a complete proposition.

(4) That more adequate provision be made for the development of improved models and new types, both as regards initial manufacturing facilities and finance.

(5) That a Board of Aeronautical Construction* be formed on the lines adumbrated in the present work, to deal with the needs of the Services and to settle specifications and approve the designs for new types, and generally to assume control and responsibility for our National Aeronautical Programme, both as to sufficiency and otherwise.

* Under the Presidency of a responsible Minister.

APPENDIX I.

THE LEWIS GUN AS AN AEROPLANE ARM.

The Lewis Machine Gun[*] has features which render it especially suitable for employment as an aeroplane arm. These are in brief:—

> The absence of water jacket.
> The lightness obtained by the adoption of pressure in place of recoil actuation.
> The self-contained magazine.

The abandonment of the water jacket is effected by resort to direct air cooling, a gilled jacket being applied to the barrel; the problem is closely analagous to that of the air cooled petrol motor. In aeronautical fighting a machine gun is never required to work continuously for any length of time, and the problem under these conditions presents no difficulty: in other fields of usefulness the reverse is the case, and calculations given later in the present appendix give some idea of the real difficulty of the problem, the solution of which has been achieved by the inventor of this weapon.

The advantage of pressure actuation in place of recoil actuation lies in the fact that if the former be adopted the total weight of the weapon can be designed to the minimum possible, whereas in a recoil actuated gun the mass of the portion which acts as "abutment" to the recoil mechanism has to be far greater than considerations of strength alone would warrant: thus the total weight is

[*] For description see "Engineering," November 8th, 1912.

App. I. APPENDIX.

greater in the older recoil actuated gun than in the Lewis type.

The importance of the self-contained magazine in a weapon to be handled from aircraft is obvious, and is so great as to make this feature almost a *sine qua non*. In the Lewis Gun each magazine contains 47 rounds, and can be replaced with but a few seconds pause in the discharge of the weapon. The resulting "breaks" in the continuity of discharge do not seriously affect the value of the arm in general usage, and in aeroplane fighting they count for nothing. The advantage, on the other hand, of a gun with no "appendages," which can be directed upward or downward or to any point of the compass at will, is one of real and decisive value.

The Problem of Direct Air Cooling. A Study of the Lewis System. Some Approximate Figures. The cooling of the barrel of a machine gun by air in place of the more usual water jacket is a problem of no mean difficulty. It is not ordinarily realised how great is the output of a machine gun in continuous firing expressed in *horse power*. Thus in the case of the M.VI service ammunition the muzzle energy is 2,000 ft. lbs.,[*] and the power represented by the energy of the stream of projectiles is approximately 0·06 horse power per shot per minute. At a maximum rate of fire of 800 per minute this gives 48 h.p. or at a normal speed of fire—say 480 per minute—29 h.p. The problem of air cooling a machine gun then, is comparable to that of air cooling an internal combustion engine, of roughly 50 b.h.p., approximately the power of an aeronautical motor such as until recently in general usage.

The comparison with an ordinary petrol motor is closer than might be supposed, since the energy and heat account, in the rifle barrel and the motor cylinder respec-

[*] M.VII ammunition is higher.

THE LEWIS GUN.   App. I.

tively, is almost identical, in spite of the diversity of the conditions. Thus the thermal efficiency in the region of 25%, in other words, about one quarter of the heat energy of the fuel on the one hand, or explosive on the other, is converted into mechanical work.*

Now we know how formidable is the difficulty of air cooling in the case of the petrol motor; the difficulty in the machine gun is augmented by the fact that the surface of the barrel on which to attach the cooling fins or gills is only about half a square foot, as compared with say two or three square feet or more in the petrol motor of equivalent output. On the other hand the condition as to temperature is not so exacting in the case of the gun barrel, and the degree of durability demanded is incomparably less.

The approximate energy account of the service rifle and ammunition is as follows:—

Kinetic energy of bullet 28%
Friction as heat imparted to bullet 5%
„ „ „   „   „ barrel 5%) Total barrel
Heat directly imparted to barrel.... 25%) heat 30%.
Kinetic and heat energy of "exhaust" powder gases 37%

100%

Thus thirty per cent. of the total heat equivalent of the charge is imparted to the barrel and has to be dispersed by the cooling means employed. The actual heat equivalent of the service charge is approximately 7,000 ft. pounds, therefore the barrel heat per charge represents 2,100 ft. pounds, and taking the ordinary maximum rate of continuous fire as 600 per minute— 10 per sec.—we have 21,000 ft. pounds per sec. as the

*Compare § 58.

App. I.   APPENDIX.

equivalent rate of heat loss; this may otherwise be expressed as

    37 Fah. H.U. per sec.
or 15 Centigrade H.U. per sec.
or 6,600 (gram) calories per sec.
or 38 horse power.

Now, the actual form taken by the cooling surface in the Lewis Gun is that of a number of radial gills of aluminium, whose aggregate surface is approximately 6 sq. ft., hence we have to dispose of the equivalent of $\frac{38}{6}$ or, say, 6 h.p. per square foot.

Following the method laid down in the author's recent "James Forrest" Lecture, the above betokens both a very considerable temperature difference and a high velocity of air over the cooling gills; the product of these (deg. Fah.) being 84,000. Thus the temperature is currently given (under the conditions in question) as about 440 deg. Fahrenheit, which means a temperature *difference* of 400 deg. Fahrenheit; this corresponds to a velocity of the air through the jacket, say, 200 ft. per second, in order that the heat shall be disposed of with sufficient rapidity by the surface of the gills.

This appears unexpectedly high, but there are two ways in which the figure may be checked. Firstly, it is clearly necessary that the total mass of air passing shall be adequate, and more than adequate, to carry off the waste heat; in other words, the air entering the jacket at the one end at atmospheric temperature must be able to absorb the whole of the waste heat before leaving the jacket, and this without its temperature being raised to such an extent as to prevent its being active as a cooling agent. Secondly, we may compare the calculated resistance of the jacket to the passage of air, with the known recoil as due to the powder gases; since the former is

THE LEWIS GUN. App. I.

overcome by the momentum of the latter, it is manifest that the jacket resistance can never exceed the mean recoil force as due to the gases: thus we have a limit to the possible velocity of the air blast.

As to the first of these, we have the combined area of the air passages, about 5 square inches, or volume per second at 200 ft. per second $= \dfrac{200 \times 5}{144} = 7$ cubic ft. $= 0.54$ lbs., equivalent in heat capacity to 0.13 lbs. of water. Now, the heat units to be taken up $= 27$, hence the air will be increased in temperature $\dfrac{27}{0.13} = 208$ Fahrenheit. This result is concordant. Evidently no velocity much less than 200 ft. a second will pass the volume necessary.

Next as to the recoil calculation. If we take the resistance of the jacket as calculable on the basis of skin-friction we may fairly assume the single surface coefficient as $.005$, and at 200 ft. per second this gives 0.3 lbs. per square foot, or, on a total surface of 6 square feet, the resistance is 1.8 lbs.; this is the mean force which must be applied by the exhaust blast of the powder gases to maintain an air current of 200 ft. per second velocity.

It has been established by experiment that the mean recoil as due to the powder gases in the service cartridge is 0.28 that of the projectile; now the latter already calculated amounts to 2 lbs. per shot per second, or 20 lbs. at 10 shots per second. Thus the mean force due to the momentum of the powder gases is $.028 \times 20 = 5.6$ lbs. But the air leaving the jacket muzzle retains approximately its mean velocity, and this represents by its momentum a force of $0.54 \times 200/32.2 = 3.35$ lbs., so the account becomes:

App. I.　　　　APPENDIX.

Cr.			Dr.		
Recoil due to powder gases	....	5·6 lbs.	Resistance of jacket ...	....	1·8 lbs.
			Efflux momentum of air	...	3·35 lbs.
			Total	....	5·15 lbs.
			Credit Balance		·45 lbs.
		5·6 lbs.			5·6 lbs.

There is, consequently, nothing inconsistent in the velocity of 200 ft. per second, though the margin of driving force as due to the momentum of the powder gases seems narrow. It is to be remembered, however, that the figure taken for the gas momentum is based on experiments made with the ordinary service rifle; it is without doubt considerably augmented by the special nozzle with which the barrel of the Lewis Gun is fitted, so that in reality there should be an ample margin.

It is worthy of note that the work done by the blast represents approximately 2 horse power, and the actual work done against the skin-friction on the gilled surface is about two-thirds of a horse power; an appreciable and valuable return for so simple an expedient as the muzzle ejector.

Summarising the foregoing, we have, under conditions firing, at 600 rounds per minute:—

1. The mean velocity of the induced air current in the cooling jacket is approximately 200 feet per second.

2. The temperature difference has a mean value of about 420 degrees Fah., that is to say the ordinary temperature of the gills is in the region of 500 Fah.

3. The momentum represented by the exhaust powder gases is a measure of the force available for

impelling the induced air current, and is consistent with the above.

In any actual measurements the jacket temperature recorded will depend very much upon where the bulb of the thermometer is placed, for there is a very steep temperature gradient from the surface of the bore of the barrel outward. Rough calculation shows that there must be a difference of about 200 degrees Fah. between the inner and outer surfaces of the barrel alone, apart from the difference in the gills themselves; thus it is improbable that the temperature of the rifled surface of the barrel when the gun is in continuous usage can be less than 700 Fah., but this does not seem to have any marked effect on its durability. Even in the case of a water cooled gun, when the water is on the boil, the internal temperature of the barrel at a high rate of fire is probably not less than 400 Fah.

The aggregate sectional area of the aluminium gills taken normal to the radius is approximately 250 sq. c. m., and the quantity of heat being 6,600 gram calories, we have the mean temperature gradient about 52 deg. C. per centimetre,* or 240 Fah. per inch (measured radially): this means a difference between the root of the gills and the outer casing of roughly 300 Fah. Hence the total difference of temperature between the outer casing and the rifling, under conditions of continuous fire, will be about 500 Fah. This is quite sufficient to give rise to uncertainty when jacket temperature is under discussion; the portion of the jacket must be specified.

* The conductivity of aluminium has been taken at 0 5 in C.G.S. Units, this is a fair average value. It is on the safe side.

APPENDIX II.

The discussion of the radius of action of aeroplanes presented in § 125 and 126, and as affecting the Naval outlook in § 128, may be helpfully illuminated by the accompanying sketch map (Fig. 21).

This map gives in outline the British Isles and the nearest adjacent portions of the Continental littoral; a few towns and places, important from the present standpoint, are indicated by their initial letters (block capitals) from which there will be no difficulty in identification.

Positions have been chosen on salient points of the Continental coast, and indicated by circles identified by numerals, thus :—

Cherbourg	is denoted by	1
The region of Calais	,, ...	2
North Holland or Texel	,, ...	3
Heligoland	,, ...	4
Stavanger (Norway)	,, ...	5

From the above points as centres, arcs of circles have been struck of 400 miles radius, as indicating the probable extreme radius or limit of raid by aeroplane. It is to be understood that raids by aeroplane at so great a radius in the face of reasonably good defensive measures will rarely be pushed home, and still more rarely successful. We may take it that any point or place in or beyond this radius is to be regarded as out of the effective reach of the enemy, and points 50 or 100 miles within this as reasonably safe. Thus, referring to the figure, station 5 may be ignored as not seriously threatening any point of importance not otherwise imperilled. The only station

NATIONAL DEFENCE.   App. II.

which brings any portion of Ireland within danger is number 1, that is to say, the French coast from Cherbourg westward. Under all conditions the region of the North Channel, including Belfast and the Clyde, and extending as far as the Naval Station at Rosyth (R on the map) may be taken as out of range.

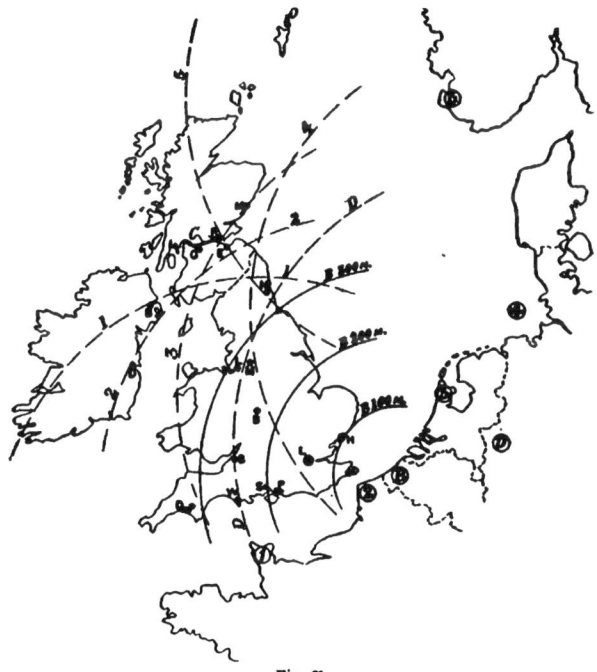

Fig. 21.

In addition to the above, the nearest point situated on the German frontier, taken to be Dusseldorf (D), has also been considered a centre of danger, and an arc of 400 miles inscribed. This brings such important centres as Newcastle, Liverpool and Manchester, Bristol and Weymouth, almost, but probably not as an actual fact

App. II. APPENDIX.

within danger. Such centres as Southampton and Portsmouth, Birmingham and the Midlands, and last but not least, London, are, however, clearly threatened.

As representing more closely the conditions of the moment, a point (B) has been taken as representing Belgian territory at present in enemy hands. From this point arcs have been struck at radii 100, 200 and 300 miles, the latter representing the probable present-day limit of raiding distance. The degree of the existing danger to our Midland and South-East Counties can be fairly judged from these indications, taken in conjunction with the discussion in the text.

The suggested ship canal from Clydebank to the Forth River is indicated in the map by the heavy line C. Apart from its strategic import, such a canal could not fail to be of great value as a commercial asset, though from that point of view alone it could not be justified to a greater extent than a mere fraction of its probable cost. Whether from a National point of view the need will justify its being carried out is a question which the future alone can determine; its strategic value would be considerable in any case, but if at any time the French littoral were to fall into enemy hands the importance of a canal such as proposed would be greatly increased.

At the moment of going to Press it has come to the author's notice that the proposal for a Ship Canal from the Firth of Forth to the West of Scotland has already been seriously considered; both the route herein suggested and an alternative route through Loch Lomond and Loch Long having received attention. For full particulars *vide* Royal Commission on Canals and Waterways; Fourth and Final Report; England, Wales and Scotland; page 183. The computed cost given in the said report, viz, twenty millions sterling, is decidedly optimistic.

INDEX.

A

Advisory Committee for Aeronautics, personnel, § 109; work of the, § 109.

Aeronautical Arm, essentially a National responsibility, § 130; future development, importance of, § 131; in peace time, § 106; must be ever ready, § 130; primary and secondary function of, § 2; strategic and tactical uses of, § 8.

Aerial and Naval Tactics contrasted, § 99.

Aeroplane, auxiliary to tactical operations, § 10; for directing artillery fire, § 10; types of machine, differentiation of, § 10; protection by armour, § 12; fighting type and its future, § 17; offensive against cavalry, § 18; attack by aeroplane on aeroplane, § 43; fighting machine as specialised type, § 44; the one-pounder as armament, § 46; attack on aeroplane, the gun supreme, § 68; aeroplane or seaplane for torpedo attack, §§ 72, 73; aeroplane and submarine, § 74; as affecting submarine activity, §§ 76, 118; present numerical weakness, §§ 1, 85; naval floating base, §§ 81, 82, 83, 84; seaplanes, the double-float and flying-boat types, §§ 79, 80; worn-out and obsolete, § 107; conditions governing size and number of bombs carried, § 117; see also **Aircraft.**

Aeroplane and Dirigible, speed limitations, § 3; range and duration of flight, § 4; analogy between air and naval forces refuted, § 5; in armed conflict, § 6; means of attack and defence, § 7; in naval reconnaissance, § 78; range and radius of action compared, § 69.

Air Fleet, need for independent combatant air fleet, § 91; must be homogeneous, § 94.

Air Power, as affecting combined tactics, § 85.

Air Raids, danger from, § 120; against city, the criterion of success, § 121; important objectives from military standpoint, § 129.

Air Tactics, § 90; formation flying, § 95.

INDEX.

Aircraft, present numerical weakness, §§ 1, 85; comparison with cavalry Arm, § 1; directing artillery fire, §§ 1, 10; in co-operation with cavalry, § 9; methods of signalling, § 10; differentiation of type, § 10; attack by rifle and gun-fire, § 11; protection by armour, § 12; offensive against cavalry, § 18; in the service of the Navy, § 69; as affecting attack and defence in combined tactics, § 87; in naval reconnaissance, relative advantages of aeroplane and dirigible, § 78; general influence on combined tactics, § 86; aeroplane bases at high altitude, § 100; landing in neutral territory, § 105; estimate of future numerical strength, § 106; merits of British machines discussed, § 108; for directing gun-fire in naval warfare, § 115; as countering submarine activity, §§ 74, 76, 118; strategic employment on large scale, § 119; see also **Aeroplane.**

Airship, see **Dirigible.**

Altitude, in reconnaissance work, §§ 9, 12; as effective against small arms fire, §§ 11, 12; difficulty of hitting aircraft by rifle or gun-fire as due to, § 11; meaning of term *high altitude*, definition, § 12; tactical value of, §§ 55, 93, 100; bases at high altitude, importance of, § 100; low altitude flying, § 13 *et seq.*

Amphibious Type of Aeroplane, utility of, § 81.

Armament, miscellaneous weapons, § 64 *et seq.*; the machine gun, §§ 15, 47, 48, 53; one-pounder, § 46; light weight shell, § 63; the bomb, §§ 64, 65; supremacy of the gun, § 68; treaty restrictions as affecting, § 45; in its relation to armour, § 54; of naval type, § 71.

Armour, and Altitude, § 12; as defence against attack from below, § 12; thickness of, § 12; penetrative power of different weapons, § 12; for low altitude and point blank range, § 14; in its relation to armament, § 54; *pros* and *cons*, § 56; and shield a distinction, § 57.

Artillery, direction of fire by aircraft, §§ 1, 10, 115; counter-aircraft, difficulties pertaining to, § 11.

Attack, from below by gun-fire, § 11; by aeroplane on other arms of the service, § 15; aeroplane on aeroplane, § 43; from above, § 56; attack and defence, balance between strategic and tactical advantages, § 86; by bomb, §§ 64, 65; on submarine, § 75; general on communications, § 119; on London or capital city, § 121 *et seq.*

B

Ballistics, the energy account, § 58.
Balloon, see **Dirigible.**

INDEX.

Balloon Hall, an unmistakable landmark, § 4.
Base, importance of altitude, § 100.
Battle Range, in naval warfare, §§ 36, 115.
Belfast and the Clyde, future importance of as seat of aeronautical and naval construction, § 126, App. II.
Board of Aeronautical Construction, advocated, §§ 113, 131.
Bomb, as a weapon of offence, § 64; difficulties of accurate aiming, the true and apparent plumb, § 65; attack on submarine by, § 75; use of in the Naval Air Service.
British Aeroplanes, points of superiority, § 108; ascendency, causes contributing to, § 109; supremacy, maintenance of, § 110.

C

Canal, proposed strategic ship canal, § 128, App. II.
Cavalry, as affected by Aeronautical Arm, §§ 9, 17, 18, 85; numerical strength of, §§ 1, 106; reconnaissance, difficulties of, § 2; future limitations of, § 18.
Clerk, (1780) writings quoted, § 39.
Clyde and Forth ship canal, suggestion for, § 128, App. II.
Combatant Air Fleet, independent air fleet and its duties, § 91.
Command of the Air, §§ 85, 88; limitations concerning, § 101; meaning of in contrast to command of the sea, § 101; strategic use of, § 119.
Communications, vulnerable to air power, § 119.
Concentration, principle of, § 19 *et seq.*
Continuity of policy, importance of, §§ 112, 131.
Counter-aircraft Artillery, facts and gunnery difficulties, § 11.

D

Danger Zone, as determined by Radius of action, § 125, App. II.
Dart, the steel dart as an aeroplane weapon, § 66.
Declaration of St. Petersburg, as affecting aeroplane armament, §§ 45, 63.
Defeat, total in air and its consequences, § 89.
Defence, aerial and naval essentially one, § 129; as affected by proximity to enemy territory, §§ 121, 125; concerning a Capital city, § 121, *et seq.*
Depreciation, and obsolescence, § 107.
Differentiation of Type, § 10.

INDEX.

Dirigible, essentially not a fighting machine, § 4; gross weights of Zeppelins, naval and military, § 4.
Dirigible and Aeroplane, see Aeroplane and Dirigible.
Distinctive National Marks, § 104.
Divided Force, weakness of, § 23 *et seq.*
Double Float Type, naval sea-plane, § 80.
Dumdum or Expanding Bullets, prohibition of, § 45; types of, § 61.
Duration and Range of Flight, aeroplane and dirigible, § 4.
Dusseldorf, raid on, § 108.

E

Energy Utilised and Lost, as determined for different weapons, §§ 58, 59.
Expanding Bullets, §§ 45, 61, 62, 63; advocated for attack on aeroplanes, §§ 45, 62; prohibition of, § 45; part played by centrifugal force in expansion, § 62.
Explosive Bullets and Projectiles, §§ 45, 50, 59, 60, 63.

F

Fighting type of Aeroplane, need for, § 2; future of, § 17; as a specialised design, § 44.
Fire, the great danger from air raid, prevention of, §§ 121, 124.
Flight Grounds, present provision unsatisfactory, § 106; night flying and, § 106.
Flight Speed, importance of, §§ 9, 92.
Floating Base, for aeroplanes and sea-planes, § 70.
Flying Boat, type of naval sea-plane, § 79.
Formation Flying, importance of, § 81; airmanship and signalling, §§ 95, 96; the "V" formation, § 97; machines disabled, § 98.
Friedrichshaven, raid on, § 103 (foot note), § 108.
Fuse, sensitive, need for, § 46.

G

Gage or Berth, advantage of upper, §§ 55, 93.
Government Manufacture, advantages and otherwise, § 111.
Gravitational Weapons, §§ 64, 65, 66.
Grenades and Bombs, § 64. See Bomb.

INDEX.

Gun-fire, ballistics of, § 58; defence from, § 12; in naval warfare difficulties of control, § 115; direction by aircraft, §§ 1, 10, 115; rapidity of fire, its importance and measure, §§ 47, 48, 49 *et seq.*; rapidity of, in relation to the *n-square* law, §§ 29, 30.

Gun, supremacy of, in attack by aircraft on aircraft, § 68.

H

High Altitude, military meaning of, § 12; bases at, value of, § 100.

Hostile Raids, defence against, §§ 120, 121; legitimate objectives, §§ 122, 129; diagram illustrating danger zone, App. II.

I

Independent Air Fleet, combatant, need for, §§ 91, 92; air tactics, §§ 92, 95; constitution of, § 94.

International Law, proper subject for, §§ 102, 103, 104; misguided views on, §§ 45, 63, 102, 105 (foot note), 123 (foot note).

Ireland, mainly out of range of hostile aircraft. National importance of Ulster industrial area, § 126, App. II.

L

Lee Gage, in naval tactics, § 39.

Lewis Gun, as an aeroplane Arm, § 15, App. I.; cooling system, calculations relating to, App. I.

London, as a capital city a legitimate object of attack, § 120; defence of, §§ 120, 123, 124.

Low Altitude Flying, advantages and disadvantages of, § 13; extreme low altitude, points in favour of, § 16.

M

Machine Gun, in the service of the Aeronautical Arm, §§ 15, 47 *et seq.*; importance of rapid fire, §§ 15, 47, 48; multiply mounted, § 41; weight of projectiles thrown by, §§ 51, 52; ammunition for, §§ 47, 48; manner of employment from aircraft, § 47; present advantages of, § 53; the Lewis gun, App. II.

Manufacture, goverment and private, § 111.

Mobilisation of Air Fleet, pontoon ship as a means for, § 81.

"Mother Ship," for aeroplanes, § 70.

INDEX.

N

N-Square Law, § 26 et seq.; demonstration of the, § 27; graphically represented, §§ 34, 35, 37; application to a heterogeneous force, § 33; examples from military history, § 32; in naval strategy and tactics, § 36 et seq.; at Trafalgar, § 42; virtual basis of Nelson's tactics, §§ 41, 42; the basis of future air tactics, §§ 81, 90, 92, 94, 95; its influence on gunnery, § 115; operation in cases of partial concentration, § 116.

Napoleon at Verona, exemplifying the *n-square law*, § 32.

National Defence, considerations relating to, § 120 et seq., App. II.

National Physical Laboratory, importance of aeronautical work of, § 102.

National Programme, recommendations respecting, § 131.

Naval and Aerial Tactics, a contrast, § 99.

Naval Aircraft, § 69 et seq.; armament of, § 71; reconnaissance, § 77.

Naval Air Service, raids carried out by, § 108.

Naval Tactics, as exemplifying the *n-square law*, §§ 39, 41, 42.

Navy, as affected by danger from hostile aircraft, § 128.

Nelson, memorandum as defining tactical scheme, § 41; his tactical scheme analysed, § 42; tactics at Trafalgar as illustrating the *n-square* law, §§ 41, 42.

Neutral Aircraft, rights and obligations, §§ 102, 103.

Neutral Territory, violation of by belligerent aircraft, §§ 103, 104, 105.

Night Flying, § 106.

Number of Aircraft, importance of numbers see *n-square* law; too small to permit of general conclusions being drawn, §§ 1, 85; in air raids, §§ 64, 117.

Numerical Strength, aircraft and cavalry compared, §§ 1, 106; and air tactics, § 90.

O

Obsolescence and Depreciation, § 107.

One-pounder, as aeroplane arm, §§ 46, 53.

P

Peace Time, conditions as affecting the aeronautical arm. Flight grounds and training, § 106.

INDEX.

Pontoon Ship, or ocean-going floating base, §§ 81, 82, 83, 84; conditions to be fulfilled by, § 82; specification of, § 83; advantages as an aeroplane base, § 84.

Primary Function, definition of, § 2; of the aeronautical Arm, § 2.

R

Radius of Action, dirigible and aeroplane compared, §§ 4, 69; as affecting danger from hostile raider, § 125, also App. II.

Raids, by air as affecting the security of the Navy, § 128; value of numerical strength, § 117; the criterion of success, § 121.

Range, see Radius of Action.

Range Finding, aircraft of known size, § 10; naval, § 115.

Rapidity of Fire, importance of, see Gun-fire.

Reconnaissance, by aircraft, § 1; tactical and strategic, § 8; by aircraft and cavalry, § 9; Naval, §§ 69, 77.

Resistance, laws of, aeroplane and dirigible, § 3.

Retreat, compelled by strategic employment of aircraft, § 119.

Rocket, considered as aeroplane weapon, 64, 67.

Rodney, early naval tactics, § 39.

Royal Aircraft Factory, work of the, § 109.

Royal Flying Corps, ascendency of the, § 108.

S

Saints, battle of, tactics at, § 39.

Scientific Investigation, importance of in aircraft development, § 109.

Sea-plane, see Aeroplane.

Secondary Function, definition, § 2; of the aeronautical Arm, § 2.

Shell, light weight, advocated by author, § 63.

Shield and Armour, comparison, § 57.

Signalling, from aircraft, §§ 10, 95.

Size, influence on resistance, § 3.

Speed, limitations, aeroplane and dirigible, § 3; as dependent upon weight per horse power, § 3.

Stability, importance of inherent stability, § 65.

Storage, aeroplane and dirigible compared, §4.

Strategic and Tactical Uses of the Aeronautical Arm, § 8.

Strategic Scout, its duties, § 9.

INDEX.

Strategic Advantage of Attack, diminished by advent of aircraft, § 86.
Strategic Employment of Aircraft, operations on a large scale, § 119.
Strategy, naval, and the n-square law, § 38.
Submarine, activity of, as affected by aircraft, §§ 75, 76, 118.
Suffren (Admiral), on naval tactics, § 39.

T

Tactical Importance of Altitude, § 93.
Tactical Operations, aircraft associated with, § 10.
Tactical Reconnaissance, § 10; conditions associated with, §§ 10, 11, 18, 44; aeroplane in the double rôle of scout and fighter, § 44.
Tactical Scheme, importance of in aerial warfare, § 90.
Tactical Uses of Aeronautical Arm, §§ 8, 10, 13 *et seq.*
Tactics, birds of prey as illustrating advantage of upper gage or berth, §§ 55, 93; naval tactics and the n-*square* law, § 39; aerial and naval contrasted, § 99; combined, as affected by aircraft, §§ 85, 86; of the air, future of, §§ 91, 92.
Torpedo, air-borne, proposed as weapon of offence, §§ 64, 67.
Torpedo, attack by air, § 72; discharge of as affecting aeroplane stability, § 73.
Trafalgar, tactical scheme as laid down in Nelson's memorandum, § 41; battle of, as illustrating the n-*square* law, § 42.
Treaty Restrictions, as affecting aircraft armament, §§ 45, 63.

U

Upper Gage, tactical importance of, §§ 55, 93.

V

"V" Formation, its value, § 97.
Villeneuve, memorandum disclosing British tactical method, § 40.

W

Warfare, ancient and modern conditions contrasted, § 20.
Weight, dirigible and aeroplane compared, § 4.

Z

Zeppelin, a failure from a military standpoint, § 131; also see **Dirigible.**

BIBLIOLIFE

Old Books Deserve a New Life
www.bibliolife.com

Did you know that you can get most of our titles in our trademark **EasyScript**™ print format? **EasyScript**™ provides readers with a larger than average typeface, for a reading experience that's easier on the eyes.

Did you know that we have an ever-growing collection of books in many languages?

Order online:
www.bibliolife.com/store

Or to exclusively browse our **EasyScript**™ collection:
www.bibliogrande.com

At BiblioLife, we aim to make knowledge more accessible by making thousands of titles available to you – quickly and affordably.

Contact us:
BiblioLife
PO Box 21206
Charleston, SC 29413

894875

Printed in Great Britain by
Amazon.co.uk, Ltd.,
Marston Gate.